I0889100

JESUS IN THE TALMUD

JESUS IN THE TALMUD

HIS PERSONALITY, HIS DISCIPLES AND HIS SAYINGS

BY

BERNHARD PICK, Ph.D. D.D.

Wipf & Stock
PUBLISHERS
Eugene, Oregon

Wipf and Stock Publishers
199 W 8th Ave, Suite 3
Eugene, OR 97401

Jesus in the Talmud
His Personality, His Disciples and His Sayings
By Pick, Bernhard
Copyright©1913 by Pick, Bernhard
ISBN: 1-59244-966-2
Publication date 10/28/2004
Previously published by Open Court, 1913

CONTENTS

PUBLISHERS' PREFACE.

The importance of the utterances in the Talmud concerning Jesus must not be misunderstood and still less must they be over-estimated. We therefore call the reader's attention to the fact that they are not based on contemporary evidence and thus possess no historical value. They are the expression of a non-Christian spirit mostly hostile and sometimes positively offensive.

In extenuation of the Talmud we must say, first, that the animosity between Jew and Gentile is deep and mutual. When the Gentile blames the Jew for wrong thinking, the Jew may equally blame the Gentile for wrong doing, for the Jew has had to suffer persecution of the cruelest kind.

Further we must bear in mind that the Talmud is not one book with a consistent tendency, but a collection of innumerable writings, essays, anecdotes, and what not. Side by side with noble and deep thoughts we find worthless gossip. On account of the latter we must not forget the former and therewith depreciate the entire Talmud.

For these reasons we wish the reader to use the present pamphlet with discretion and to bear in mind the conditions existing in the age in which these utterances concerning Jesus were written. The author has collected and collated them for serious study of the facts in the case. They are material for the scholar and must not in any sense be considered as popular reading.

THE PUBLISHERS.

NOTE BY THE AUTHOR.—The greater part of this work was already in print when the interesting book of Prof. Starck was published. Jesus Die Härstiker und die Christen, Leipzig, 1910.

PART I.

PERSONALITY OF JESUS.

I.

THE TALMUD.

Introduction.—Jesus as represented in the Talmud is a subject which must interest the Christian student. For what can be of profounder interest than to learn what the Jews have said concerning Jesus and Christianity. We naturally look to the Jewish historian Josephus, who described and witnessed the downfall of the Jewish commonwealth. But we are disappointed. True that in his "Antiquities" (XVIII, 3, 3) Josephus has reference to Christ, but scholars are now generally agreed[1] that this passage is a later interpolation. Leaving then aside Josephus, we must turn to that encyclopedia of "Jewish wisdom and unwisdom" which is known as the Talmud. We cannot speak here of the origin and contents of this voluminous work, of which a complete translation into any modern language does not yet exist. We must refer the reader to

[1] See however among other defenders of the passage in Josephus, Seitz, *Christus-Zeugnisse aus dem klassischen Altertum,* Cologne, 1906, 9 et. seq.

our article "Talmud."[2] But even this work does not add anything to our knowledge, yea, it is rather disappointing. For the Talmud as we now have it contains not those Christian or rather anti-Christian passages, which it originally had.

Modern Judaism complains of the intolerance of the Church, which from the time of Justinian[3] persecuted and burned the Talmud. But it forgets that the Talmud only reaped what it has sowed, and that the Church of Rome only acted in accordance with the Talmud itself. For it was the very Talmud which taught that in case of a fire breaking out on the Sabbath, the Gospels and other works of the *minim* (i. e., Christians) should not be rescued. "By the life of my son," said the Rabbi Tarphon, "should they (i. e., these writings) come into my hand I would burn them together with the names of God which they contained. Were I pursued, I would rather take refuge in a temple of idols than in their (i. e., the Christians') houses. For the latter are wilful traitors, while the heathen sinned in ignorance of the right way; and concerning them the Scripture says: 'Behind the doors, also, and the posts, hast thou set up thy

[2] See McClintock & Strong's *Theol. Enc.*, vol. X (1881) *s. v.* "Talmud."

[3] On February 13, 553, he issued a novella "concerning the Jews."

remembrance' " (Is. lvii. 8).[4] This fact should not be forgotten.

The anti-Christian character of Jewish writings early attracted the attention of Christians, and Agobard, bishop of Lyons (820-830) in his *De Judaicis Superstitionibus,* and Hrabanus Maurus, archbishop of Mayence, in his *Contra Judaeos,* written about 847 A. D., betray acquaintance with Jewish literature. The first attack upon the Talmud was made in the thirteenth century, when A. D. 1240 a conference was held at Paris between Nicolas Donin and some Jewish rabbis. When the question came up as to Jesus in the Talmud, rabbi Jechiel, the most prominent of the Jewish rabbis at that conference, would not admit that the Jesus spoken of in the Talmud was Jesus of Nazareth, but another Jesus, a discovery which was copied by some later writers. But modern Jews acknowledge the failure of this argument, for says Dr. Levin in his prize essay: "We must regard the attempt of rabbi Jechiel to ascertain that there were two by the name of Jesus as unfortunate, original as the idea may be."[5] As the author of this essay

[4] Talmud, *Shabbath,* fol. 116, col. 1. This his animosity against Christianity induced some scholars to maintain that this Rabbi Tarphon is the same Trypho who is the interlocutor in Justin Martyr's *Dialogue.*

[5] "Die Religionsdisputation des Rabbi Jechiel von Paris," published in Graetz's *Monatsschrift,* Breslau, 1869, p. 193.

was a pupil of the rabbinical seminary at Breslau, he certainly expressed the opinion of his teachers. The result of the conference was that the Talmud in wagon-loads was burned at Paris in 1242.

In our days, such accusations against the Talmud were impossible, because all these offensive passages have been removed—not so much by the hands of the Christian censor, as by the Jews themselves—a fact very often overlooked by controversialists. In the Jewish year 5391 (i. e., A. D. 1631) a Jewish synod held at Petrikau, in Poland, issued a circular letter[6] to the effect that all such passages in the Talmud which refer to Jesus etc., should be omitted in the future. This letter explains the absence of those offensive passages from the editions of the Talmud published since the publication of the Amsterdam edition in 1644. But happily or unhappily the Jews themselves have taken care that "the expurgated passages in the Talmud" did not become lost to their coreligionists by publishing them anonymously in pamphlets, of which Professor Strack of Berlin mentions no less than four such editions.[7] These collections, published

[6] The reader can find this circular letter in my article "Talmud" in McClintock & Strong's *Theol. Enc.*, vol. x, p. 172.

[7] The present writer has also one of these collections, published in Cracow, 1893.

for the most part in Germany, are of a recent date, and are probably intended for more than a mere literary interest.

In order to give back to the Jews what the censor has taken from them and to show them that Christianity has nothing to fear from these expurgated passages, Professor Dalman of Leipsic, one of the few Christian scholars who are entitled to be heard even in *Talmudicis*, has published in a convenient form all these passages contained in the oldest editions of the Talmud and Midrash. To this collection of the censured passages H. Laible appended an introductory essay, and the whole was published under the title *Jesus Christus im Talmud,* Berlin, 1891, by the missionary "Institutum Judaicum."

Before we enter into the debating club of the rabbis, we shall make a few preliminary remarks which can prepare us for the Talmudic statements.

During the life-time of Jesus his miracles were not denied but were traced back to Beelzebub, the prince of the devils (Mark iii. 22). The scribes would not recognize one who sought not their company, but that of publicans and sinners with whom he ate; who broke the Sabbath and abolished the difference between clean and unclean. That the grave of Christ had been empty, the Jews did not deny, but they thought that the disciples had stolen the body (Matt. xxviii. 15). They freely made use of the invective Beelzebub ("master of the house") for the "master" of the Christians as well as for his servants (Matt. x. 25). After his death, the crucified Messiah, as Paul tells us, became unto them a stumbling block (1 Cor. 1, 23). The destruction of Jerusalem had made no impression upon "these villains" and upon "that ungodly generation," as Josephus calls his countrymen (*War,* v, 13, 6). But if the sword of Judaism was perforce sheathed, its tongues and pens were active. The apologetic writings of the earliest centuries, show that the Jews were busy throughout this whole era in circulating calumnies against the Christians. Justin Martyr (died 163 A. D.) complains of the Jewish blasphemies against Christ and the Christians. "The high priests of your nation and your teachers," he says, "have caused that the name of Jesus should be profaned and reviled through the whole world" (*Dialogue with Trypho,* 117). "Nay, ye have added thereto, that Christ taught those impious, unlawful, horrible actions, which ye disseminate as charges above all against those who acknowledge Christ as Teacher and as the Son of God" (*ibid,* 108). "Your teachers exhort you to permit yourselves no conversation whatever with us" (*ibid.* 112). "The Jews regard us as foes and opponents, and kill, and torture us if they have the power. In the lately-ended Jewish war, Bar Kokh'ba, the instigator of the Jewish revolt, caused Christians alone to be dragged to terrible tortures, whenever they would not deny and revile Jesus Christ" (*Apology,* I, 31). "The Jews hate us, because we say that Christ is already come, and because we point out that He, as had been prophesied, was crucified by them" (*Dial.* 35). "Ye have killed the Just and His prophets before Him. And now ye despise those who hope in Him and in God, the King over all and Creator of all things, who has sent Jesus; ye despise and dishonor them, as much as in you lies, in that in your synagogues ye curse those who believe in Christ. Ye only lack the power, on account of those who hold the reins of government, to treat us with violence. But as often as ye have had this power, ye have also done this" (*ibid.* 16). "In your synagogues ye curse all who have become Christians, and the same is done by the other nations, who give a practical turn to the curse, in that when any one acknowledges himself a Christian, they put him to death" (*ibid.* 96).

From the "True Word" of Celsus, which has been answered by Origen, we already learn some of the mean things which the Jews circulated about Jesus. The Jew whom Celsus introduces charges Jesus with having falsely proclaimed himself to be born of a virgin; afterwards he says that Jesus was born in a poor Jewish village, and that his mother was a poor woman of the country, who supported herself with spinning and needlework; that she was cast off by her betrothed, a carpenter; and that after she was rejected by her husband, she wandered about in disgrace and misery till she secretly gave birth to Jesus. Jesus himself was obliged from poverty and necessity to go down as servant into Egypt, where he learnt some of the secret sciences which are in high honor among the Egyptians; and he placed such confidence in these sciences that on his return to his native land he gave himself out to be a god (I, 28). The Jew of Celsus also declares that the carpenter who was betrothed to Mary, put the mother of Jesus from him, because she had broken faith with him, in favor of a soldier named Panthera (I, 32).

Tertullian writing somewhere about 197-198 A. D. in his *De Spectaculis,* chap. 30, in which he depicts the glorious spectacle of the second coming says that he will turn to the Jews who raged against the Lord and say unto them: "This is your carpenter's son, your harlot's son; your sabbath-breaker, your Samaritan, your demon-possessed! This is He whom ye bought from Judas; this is He who was struck with reeds and fists, dishonored with spittle, and given a draught of gall and vinegar! This is He whom His disciples have stolen secretly, that it may be said He has risen, or the gardener abstracted that his lettuces might not be damaged by the crowds of visitors!"

Such is already the attitude of Judaism towards Jesus at a time when the Talmud was in a state of formation. But if we wish to become acquainted with the Rabbinical Jesus-tradition we must examine the constituent parts of the Talmud, namely the Mishna, Tosephta (i. e., addition or supplement to the Mishna), the Gemara or commentary on the Mishna, and the Midrashim or homiletic literature, especially the Midrash Kohelet or Midrash on Ecclesiastes. The Talmudic Jesus traditions continued themselves even after the time of the completion of the Talmud. They were further developed and enlarged, and reached their full expression in the Middle Ages. In that period the hatred of Jesus which was never quite dormant, begat a literature, in comparison with which the Talmud must be termed almost innocent. The Toldoth Jeshu literature originated, which is still continued. In the Toldoth Jeshu a detailed picture of the life of Jesus was put together, of which the authors of the Talmud had no anticipation. The three consonants *j s* (*shin*) *v,* with which the name

Jeshu was written, are here explained as being the first letters of the three words: *j* = *jimmach, sh* = *sh'mo, v* = *v'zichro,* i. e., "may be blotted out his name and his memory"! The Toldoth Jeshu is nothing but the offspring of low fanaticism, malicious delight in defamation, and vulgar imagination which respectable Jews have always despised.

After these preliminaries we now take up the passages of the Talmud as given by Dalman, and which are claimed to refer to Jesus.

II.

THE PERSONALITY OF JESUS.

Birth and Parentage of Jesus.—In the Talmud Shabbath 104^b we read: "He who cuts upon his flesh." It is a tradition that Rabbi Eliezer said to the wise, Has not Ben Stada brought magic spells from Egypt in a cut which was upon his body? They answered him, He was a fool, and we do not take proofs from fools. [Ben Stada is Ben Pandira. Rab Hisda said, The husband was Stada, the paramour was Pandira. The husband was Paphos ben Jehudah, the mother was Stada. The mother was Miriam the dresser of women's hair, as we say in Pumbeditha, Such a one has been false to her husband.][8]

The above passage occurs in a discussion upon the words in the Mishnah which forbid all kinds of writing to be done on the Sabbath. Several

[8] The passage in [] which also occurs in Sanhedrin 67*a*, is not found in modern editions. It is supplied from Rabbinowicz Diqduqé Sopherim, on the authority of the Munich and Oxford manuscripts, and the older editions.

kinds are specified, and among them the making of marks upon the flesh. The words at the beginning of the translation, "he who cuts upon his flesh," are the text, so to speak, of the Mishnah which is discussed in what follows. To illustrate the practice of making marks on the skin, the compilers of the Gemara introduce a tradition, according to which Rabbi Eliezer asked the question, "Did not Ben Stada bring magical spells from Egypt in a cut which was upon his body?" His argument was that as Ben Stada had done this, the practice might be allowable. The answer was that Ben Stada was a fool, and his case proved nothing. Upon the mention however of Ben Stada, a note is added to explain who that person was, and it is for the sake of this note that the passage is quoted.

The two names Ben Stada and Ben Pandera evidently refer to the same person, and that that person is Jesus is shown clearly by the fact that we sometimes meet with the full name "Jeshu son of Pandera," also Jeshu son of Stada." It seems that the question was argued in the schools which of the two familiar designations (son of Stada, son of Pandera) was the correct one. One of the two appellations appeared to be necessarily false. Which was correct?

The subject treated was that the son of Stada had brought charms with him out of Egypt in an incision in his flesh. Thereupon some one objects; the designation Ben Stada is false; he was the son of Pandera. No, says Rab Hisda (a Babylonian teacher, A. D. 217-309), Stada was the name of the husband (of his mother), Pandira the name of her paramour. To call him either the one or the other is therefore correct. To this however is objected that this cannot be true, because the husband is known to have been called Paphos ben Jehudah. Stada must have been not the father but the mother. But how can that be, because the mother was called Miriam the dresser of women's hair? As rejoinder to this follows the conclusion: Of what we are aware, but she is also called Stada, by her nickname. Insomuch as she had a paramour, she was given the "sobriquet" Stada, which consists of the words *stath da,* i. e., she has gone aside, from her husband. Thus at least the word is explained in the Babylonian Academy at Pumbeditha.

Various attempts have been made to explain the two names Ben Stada and Ben Pandira (also written Pandera or Pantira). But none of the suggested explanations solves the problem. We leave the two names as relics of ancient Jewish mockery against Jesus, the clue to whose meaning is now lost.

Mention has also been made of Miriam (of which Mary is the equivalent). She is called *m'gaddla nashaia,* i. e., a women's hairdresser. How came the Talmud to bestow this epithet upon the mother of Jesus, for whom elsewhere it has the characteristic designation of adulteress? That Jesus's mother was named Mary, was known to the Jews; that she had born Jesus out of wedlock, was maintained by them. Then they heard a noted Christian woman of Jesus's time often spoken of, who was named Mary of Magdala. What was more natural for those who had already long ceased to ascertain more particularly at the mouth of Christians the history of Jesus, than by this Mary (of) Magdala simply to understand Jesus's mother, especially since their knowledge was confined to one Mary? She was reported to be a great sinner. This harmonized in a twofold way with their assumption, for, that Jesus's mother was a sinner, was maintained by them with the utmost certainty, and now they obtained, as they supposed, actual confirmation of this from the Christians. Miriam (of) Magdala was accordingly the mother of Jesus, and by a name-play the Magdala was turned into *m'gaddla nashaia,* i. e., women's hairdresser.

In the Talmudic passage quoted above we are told that Stada's (i. e., Mary's) lawful husband was Paphos ben Jehudah. Now of this Paphos, who lived a century after Jesus, the Talmud Gittin 90[a] narrates the following:

"There is a tradition, Rabbi Meir used to say; 'Just as there are various kinds of taste as regards eating, so there are also various dispositions as regards women. There is a man into whose cup a fly falls and he casts it out, but all the same he does not drink it [the cup]. Such was the manner of Paphos ben Jehudah, who used to lock the door upon his wife, and go out.' "

All we learn from this passage directly with regard to Paphos ben Jehudah, a contemporary of Rabbi Akiba, is that he locked up his wife; we are, however, led to conclude, indirectly, that she ultimately proved unfaithful to her tyrannical spouse. What, then, was more simple than for a story-teller to connect this with the details of unfaithfulness found in his Jeshu repertoire? The erring wife was just like Miriam; before long she actually became Miriam, and finally Paphos ben Jehudah was confidently given as Miriam's husband! So they had it in later times, and the great Talmudic commentator Rashi (died A. D. 1105) comments thus upon our passage: "Paphos ben Jehudah was the husband of Mary, the women's hairdresser. Whenever he went out of his house into the street, he locked the door upon her, that no one might be able to speak with her. And that is a course which became him not; for on this account there arose enmity between them, and she in wantonness broke her faith with her husband."

A Mary Legend.—In the Talmud Hagigah 4[b] we read the following: "When Rab Joseph came to this verse (Prov. xiii. 23), 'But there is that is destroyed without judgment,' he wept. He said: 'Is there really some one who is going [away], when it is not his time?' None but this [told] of Rab Bibi bar Abbai. The Angel of Death was with him. The Angel said to his messenger, 'Go bring me Miriam the dresser of women's hair.' He brought him Miriam the teacher of children. He [the Angel] said, 'I told thee Miriam the dresser of women's hair.' He said, 'If so, I will take this one back.' He said, 'Since thou has brought this one, let her be among the number [of the dead].'"

In this narrative we have a monstrous anachronism. Rab Joseph, who is mentioned here, was born at Shiti, in Babylonia, A. D. 259 and died in 325. Rab Bibi flourished in the fourth century. The latter can neither have seen Mary nor have been her contemporary. The Talmudic commentary Tosaphoth remarks: "The Angel of Death was with him: he related what had already happened, for this about Miriam the dresser of women's hair took place in [the time of] the second temple, for she was the mother of that *so* and *so* [i. e., Jesus], as it is said in Shabbath 104[b]." But the wording of the Talmud says quite distinctly that Mary lived in the very time of Rab Bibi, on which account the Angel of Death spoke with him not of one who had existed earlier, but of one actually living. Further this angel, we may note, at that very time in the presence of Rab Bibi commissions his messenger, to bring her i. e., deliver her to death. The Tosaphoth notes on Shabbath 104^b seek needlessly to remove the anachronism by the assumption that there were two women's hair-dressers, named Mary. But this attempt is in vain, for nothing is known of that second Mary. Besides we must not forget that the Talmud, in relation to Jesus, has no conception of chronology, and indeed, the later the origin of notices about Jesus, the more reckless are they in their chronological lapses. The post-Talmudic Second Targum on the Book of Esther actually reckons Jesus among the ancestors of Haman, an anachronism, which Levy in his Targumic dictionary (I, 330) seeks in vain to justify. In the face of such an unfathomable error what signifies the erroneous representation that Rab Bibi lived in the time of Mary?

III.

JESUS ALLEGED TO BE BORN OUT OF WEDLOCK.

The Pretended Record.—It is said in Mishnah Jebamoth iv. 13[9] (Gemara 49[b]): "Simeon ben Azai said, 'I have found in Jerusalem a book of genealogies, and therein is written: That *so and so*[10] is a *mamzer*[11] of a married woman, to confirm the words of Rabbi Jehoshua.'"

This passage is from the Mishnah, and therefore belongs to the older stratum of the Talmud. Ben Azai flourished at the end of the first and the beginning of the second century, and was a friend and contemporary of Rabbi Akiba who was a particularly zealous opponent of the Chris-

[9] It is interesting that the English translators of the Eighteen Treatises of the Mishna, rabbis De Sola and Raphall (London, 1845) have not translated this part of the fourth chapter. Why?

[10] The original reads *peloni*, and is one of the twenty-eight periphrastic titles of Jesus from Jewish writings, adduced by Eisenmenger in the second chapter of the first part of his *Entdecktes Judenthum.*

[11] i. e., a bastard, a predicate attributed by the Jews to Jesus.

tians. When Ben Azai reported that he had found a book of pedigrees, in which it was stated that *so and so* (peloni) was of spurious birth, it is certainly probable that reference is to Jesus. Unless some well-known man were intended, there would no point in referring to him; and unless there had been some strong reason for avoiding his name, the name would have been given in order to strengthen the argument founded upon the case. For it is said that Ben Azai made his statement in order "to confirm the words of Rabbi Joshua." The matter in question concerned the definition of the notion of *mamzer,* a predicate which the Jews only too willingly ascribed to Jesus. That the passage refers to Jesus is admitted by the Jewish scholar J. Derenbourg (in *Revue des Etudes Juives,* III, 293, n. 3).

Alleged Confession by the Mother of Jesus. In the treatise Kallah 18^b we read the following: "A shameless person is according to Rabbi Eliezer a bastard, according to Rabbi Joshua a son of woman in her separation, according to Rabbi Akiba a bastard *and* son of a woman in her separation. Once there sat elders at the gate when two boys passed by; one had his head covered, the other bare. Of him who had his head uncovered Rabbi Eliezer said, 'a bastard!' Rabbi Joshua said, 'A son of a woman in her separation!' Rabbi Akiba said, 'A bastard *and* son of a woman in her separation!' They said to Rabbi Akiba, 'How has thine heart impelled thee to the audacity of contradicting the words of thy colleagues?' He said to them, 'I am about to prove it. Thereupon he went to the boy's mother, and found her sitting in the market and selling pulse. He said to her, 'My daughter, if thou tellest me the thing which I ask thee, I will bring thee to eternal life.' She said to him, 'Swear it to me! Thereupon Rabbi Akiba took the oath with his lips, while he canceled it in his heart. Then said he to her, 'Of what sort is this thy son?' She said to him, 'When I betook myself to the bridal chamber, I was in my separation, and my husband stayed away from me. But my paranymph [i. e., the bridegroom's best man] came to me, and by him I have this son.' So the boy was discovered to be both a bastard and the son of a woman in her separation. Thereupon said they, 'Great is Rabbi Akiba, in that he has put to shame his teachers.' In the same hour they said, 'Blessed be the Lord God of Israel who has revealed this secret to Rabbi Akiba ben Joseph.' "

This famous discussion on bastardy, even when taken by itself, is remarkable from the ethical point of view. Considering the strange ascription of an act of heartless perjury to Akiba as the means whereby he extorted the confession from the boy's mother, and the far more curious addition at the end of the passage which blesses the God of Israel for revealing "this secret" after the use of such questionable means, we ask: Can modern Jews still uphold the reputation of the Talmud or of its great authority, Akiba?

Considering the passage by itself, we see that neither the name of the son nor that of the mother is here mentioned. But the fact that use has been made of the story in the *Toldoth Jeshu* (ed. Hulreich, p. 22; ed. Wagenseil, p. 12; MS. Strassburg, ed. Krauss,[12] p. 39; MS. Vindobona, *ibid.*, p. 69) shows that it was regarded as having reference to Jesus. That Akiba lived about a century after Jesus, is of no account, since the Talmud abounds in anachronisms.

Jesus and His Teacher.—Whereas the New Testament knows nothing of Jesus having enjoyed the tuition of a rabbi, the Talmud *Sanhedrin,* 107*b* (and almost exactly in the same words *Sota,* 47*a*) narrates the following: "Our Rabbis teach, Ever let the left hand repel and the right hand invite, not like Elisha who repulsed Gehazi with both hands, and not like Rabbi Joshua ben Perachjah who repulsed Jeshu (the Nazarene) with both hands. What of Rabbi Joshua ben Perachjah? When Jannai the king

[12] *Das Leben Jesu nach jüdischen Quellen,* Berlin, 1902.

killed our Rabbis, Joshua ben Perachjah [and Jeshu] fled to Alexandria in Egypt. When there was peace, Simon ben Shetach wrote to him: 'From me [Jerusalem] the city of holiness, to thee Alexandria of Egypt [my sister]. My husband stays in thy midst and I sit forsaken.' He came and found himself at a certain inn; they showed him great honor. He said, 'How beautiful is this Ascania![13] [Jesus] said to him, 'Rabbi, she has narrow eyes.' He said, 'Wretch, dost thou employ thyself thus?' He sent out 400 trumpets and excommunicated him. He [Jesus] came before him many times and said to him, 'Receive me.' But he would not notice him. One day he [i. e., Joshua] was reciting the Shema (i. e., the words: 'Hear, O Israel,' Deut. vi. 4 et seq.), he [i. e., Jesus] came before him. He was minded to receive him, and made a sign to him. He [i. e., Jesus] thought that he repelled him. He went and hung up a tile and worshiped it. Joshua said to him, 'Return.' He replied, 'Thus I have received from thee, that every one who sins and causes the multitude to sin, they give him not the chance to repent.' And the teacher [i. e., he who has handed down this tradition] has said, 'Jesus

[13] The word means both inn and innkeeper. Joshua uses it in the first sense, the answering remark implies the second meaning "hostess."

the Nazarene practiced magic and led astray and deceived Israel.' "[14]

In the Jerusalem Talmud *Hagigah, 77d,* the same story is related only that in place of Joshua ben Perachjah his contemporary Judah ben Tabbai is placed and that the name of Jesus is not mentioned, for which we read "one of his (Tabbai's) disciples." But whether the reading is Joshua ben Perachjah or Judah ben Tabbai we have here again one of those striking anachronisms for which the Talmud is famous. The event under King Jannai (i. e., Alexander Jannaeus) is historical. After the capture of the stronghold Bethome King Jannai (104-78 B. C.) had 800 Pharisees crucified. This crucifixion was the occasion of the flight into Syria and Egypt on the part of the Pharisees generally in the country, and among them Joshua ben Perachjah and Judah ben Tabbai. The question may be asked, how did the name of Jesus[15] come to be introduced into a story referring to a time so long before his own? Bearing in mind that the rabbis had extremely vague ideas of the chronology of past times, we may perhaps find

[14] This formal charge is also found in *Sanhedrin* 43*a*, where the words of "the teacher" are found.

[15] In the edition of Basel, 1578-81, and in all later ones, the censor of the press has expunged the name of Jesus, which is found in all the older editions of the Talmud.

the origin of the story in its Babylonian form in a desire to explain the connection of Jesus with Egypt. The connecting link may, perhaps, be found in the fact of a flight into Egypt to escape the anger of a king. This was known in regard to Joshua ben Perachjah, and the Gospel (Matt. ii. 13 et seq.) records a similar event in regard to Jesus. There may be some other details in the life of Jesus which the rabbis had in view when they remodeled the story to suit their purpose. Hence, in rejecting the date, it is not absolutely necessary to reject the whole of the Babylonian version as entirely devoid of every element of genuineness. Again, as to the lateness of the Babylonian version, it is to be observed that the Gemara quotes from an earlier source or tradition of the story, as can be seen from the closing words of the Talmud passage (*Sanhedrin* 107*b*) given above.

Jesus a Magician.—Whereas the Toldoth Jeshu attributes the miraculous power of Jesus to the Shem (i. e., the Tetragrammaton or Ineffable Name) which he stole from the Temple at Jerusalem by a strange device, the Talmud knows nothing of this robbing of the Shem from the Temple, but records that Jesus brought magic out of Egypt.[16] The passages referring to it are:

[16] Egypt was regarded as the special home of magic, an opinion expressed in the Talmud Kiddushin 49*b*: "Ten measures of sorcery descended into the world, Egypt received nine, the rest of the world one."

1. Tosephta[17] Shabbath XII: "He who upon the Sabbath cuts letters upon his body is, according to the view of Rabbi Eliezer guilty, according to the view of the sages he is not guilty. Rabbi Eliezer said to the sages: 'Ben Stada surely learned sorcery by such writing.' They replied to him: 'Should we in any wise on account of a fool destroy all reasonable men?' "

2. Jerusalem Shabbath 13*d*: 'He who scratches on the skin in the fashion of writing is guilty, but he who makes marks on the skin in the fashion of writing is exempt from punishment. Rabbi Eliezer said to them: 'But has not Ben Stada brought magic spells out of Egypt in this way?' They answered him: 'On account of one fool we do not ruin a multitude of reasonable men.' "

3. Shabbath 104*b*: "It is a tradition that Rabbi Eliezer said to the sages: 'Did not Ben Stada bring spells from Egypt in a cut which was upon his flesh?' They replied: 'He was a fool, and they do not bring a proof from a fool.' "

It has already been shown above that Ben Stada denotes Jesus. In the passages before us he is charged with bringing magical charms from Egypt concealed in an incision in his flesh. The charge that he was a magician is no doubt based on the belief that he did many miracles, a belief which found ample support in the Gospel records.

[17] That is "supplement to the Mishna"; best edition by Zuckermandel, (Pasewalk, 1880), p. 126.

To say that Jesus learned magic in Egypt, the special home of magic according to the Talmud Kiddushin 49*b* already referred to, is to say that he was a great magician, more powerful than others. That he had something to do with Egypt we have also seen above in the passage which makes him a disciple of Joshua ben Perachjah. As to the manner in which he is alleged to have brought with him Egyptian magic, a curious explanation is given by Rashi, the Talmud commentator on Shabbath 104*b* to the effect that "the Egyptian magicians searched every one who quitted the land of Egypt, whether he was taking any books of magic with him, in order that the magical art (namely, the Egyptian) might not come into other countries." Now since Jesus could not take them away in writing, he concealed them in the manner described, or perhaps tatooed magical signs on his flesh.

Jesus An Idolater.—Jesus is not only a fool but also an idolator. In the Talmud Sanhedrin 103*a* we read on the passage Ps. xci. 10, "There shall no evil befall thee," that it means that evil dreams and bad fantasies shall not vex thee; on "Neither shall any plague come nigh thy tent," that it means that thou shalt not have a son or disciple who burns his food publicly like Jeshu (i. e., Jesus) the Nazarene.[18]

[18] So in all the older editions and the manuscripts.

The last clause is also found in Talmud Berachoth 17*b*. The authority who quotes this passage is Rabbi Hisda, a Babylonian who lived A. D. 217-309. He quotes it in the name of Rabbi Jeremiah bar Abba, who was his contemporary, and apparently of about the same age. As to the term "to burn his food publicly," lexicographers are of different opinions. Dalman says that this means "to renounce publicly what one has learned." Laible thinks that the term is "a contemptuous expression for the public offering of sacrifice to idols. That the Christians in their assemblies offered sacrifice to idols was as firmly the opinion of the Jews of olden time as it is that of many of the present day. Naturally, therefore, it was concluded that Jesus must have commenced it." May be it refers to the fact that Jesus went and taught the people publicly—the poor, the outcast, the oppressed, the sinners, the publicans, in a word the unpurified people, with whom a disciple of a rabbi ought not to associate. But whatever the meaning, certain it is that in the eyes of the rabbis Jesus was a heterodox, who according to Talmud Sanhedrin 43*a* and 107*b* "corrupted and seduced Israel."

Claim of Jesus Denied.—In the Jerusalem Talmud Taanith 65*b* we read with reference to Num. xxiii. 19: "Rabbi Abahu said, If a man shall say to thee, 'I am God,' he lies; if he says,

'I am the son of man,' he shall rue it; 'I will go up to heaven' (to this applies Num. xxiii. 19) he saith, but shall not perform it."

That the passage refers to Jesus there can be no possibility of doubt. This Rabbi Abahu, who lived in Cæsarea at the end of the third and the beginning of the fourth century, seems to have largely engaged in controversy with Jewish Christians. According to Abahu any one who says that he is God and at the same time designates himself as Son of Man—and this no man save Jesus has ever done—is a liar.

The import of the testimony of Jesus to Himself is mentioned also in the Midrash Pesikta Rabbathi (ed. Freidmann, 1880), fol. 100*b*: "Rabbi Hia bar Abba [about 216 A. D.] said: 'If the son of the harlot shall say to thee, There be two Gods, answer him, I am He of the sea, I am He of Sinai.' Rabbi Hia bar Abba said, 'If the son of the harlot shall say to thee, There be two Gods, answer him, It is here (Deut. v. 4) written not *Gods* but *the Lord* hath spoken with you face to face.' "

That God has a son, and that for this reason there are two Gods, passes here for the teaching of the harlot's son, wherein the reference is clear, namely to Jesus.

An amplification of Abahu's work, given above, is found in the Midrash Jalqut Shimoni (also

Midrash Jelammedenu) on Num. xxiii. 7, where we read that Rabbi Eleazar ha-Qappar said that "God gave strength to his (Balaam's) voice, so that it went from one end of the world to the other, because he looked forth and beheld the peoples that bow down to the sun and moon and stars, and to wood and stone, and he looked forth and beheld that there was a man, son of a woman, who should rise up and seek to make himself God, and to cause the whole world to go astray. Therefore God gave power to his voice that all the peoples of the world might hear, and thus he spake, 'Give heed that ye go not astray after that man, for it is written (Num. xxiii. 19), 'God is not a man that he should lie,' and if he says that he is God he is a liar, and he will deceive and say that he departeth and cometh again in the end, he saith and he shall not perform. See what is written (Num. xxvi. 23): 'And he took up his parable and said, Alas, who shall live when he makes (himself) God!' Balaam intended to say, Alas, who shall live of that nation which heareth that man who hath made himself God."—

Now Eleazar ha-Qappar, who is reported to have said all this, was earlier than Abahu, for he died about 260 A. D. Whether all is to be taken as Qappar's work, we know not. At all events we have here a naive prophecy after the event, which makes Balaam quote his own words (Num.

xxiii. 19) as scripture. One thing however is certain: Jesus is here referred to more fully than in the shorter saying of Abahu.

Balaam-Jesus.—In Mishna Sanhedrin x, 2, we read: "Three kings and four private men have no part in the world to come. The three kings are Jeroboam, Ahab and Manasseh. . . . the four private men are Balaam, Doeg, Ahitophel and Gehazi."

This passage belongs to the famous chapter of the Mishna, entitled *Chelek*, because it commences by saying that "all Israel have part (*chelek*) in the world to come," and then enumerates the exceptions. The three kings, Jeroboam, Ahab and Manasseh are all mentioned in the Old Testament as having introduced idolatry, perverted the true religion. The immediate connection of the four private persons arouses the conjecture that they were condemned for the same offense. This conclusion is strengthened by the fact that the preceding paragraph of the Mishna (x, 1) in this chapter excepts from the privilege of the world to come according to Rabbi Akiba also such a person "who reads in external books and who whispers over a wound, and says, None of the diseases which I sent in Egypt will I lay upon thee, I the Lord am thy healer." Now the external books, according to the Gemara upon this passage (fol. 100*b*) are the *Siphre Minim,* i. e., the books of the Jewish Christians or Christians generally, which books by way of caricature Rabbi Meïr (130-160 A. D.) calls *awen gillayon* (literally, margin of evil) and Rabbi Jochanan (Meïr's contemporary) calls *awon gillayon* (i. e., blank paper of sin)—thus in Talmud Shabbath 116*a* (MS. Munich).

The words "who whispers over a wound, refer to the miraculous cures of the Christians.

The combination of Balaam with Doeg, Ahitophel and Gehazi is certainly extraordinary. Balaam was not an Israelite, and therefore could not logically be included in a list of exceptions to a rule which only affected Israelites. It is evident that Balaam here does not mean the ancient prophet of Num. xxii et seq., but some one else for whom that ancient prophet could serve as a type. From the Jewish point of view there was considerable likeness between Balaam and Jesus. Both had led the people astray; and if the former had tempted them to gross immorality, the latter, according to the Rabbis, had tempted them to gross apostasy. This was the great charge against Jesus, that "he practised magic and deceived and led astray Israel." If it be true that Balaam stands for Jesus, then it is reasonable to suppose that Doeg, Ahitophel and Gehazi stand for the names of some other persons who had fallen under severe Rabbinical displeasure. Who they were precisely we have now no means of discovering, and the supposition that they refer to Peter, James and John, or Peter, Judas Iscariot[19] and Paul may be possible. However this may be, the rabbis were convinced that the disciples of Balaam *en bloc* would inherit Gehenna, as we read in Aboth v. 19: "The disciples of our father Abraham enjoy this world and inherit the world to come, as it is written (Prov. viii. 21) 'That I may cause those that love me to inherit substance, and that I may fill their treasuries.' The disciples of Balaam the impious inherit Gehenna and go down into the pit of destruction, as it is written (Ps. lv. 24): 'But thou, O God, shalt bring them down into the pit of destruction; bloodthirsty and deceitful men shall not live out half their days:' "

And if there should by any chance be still the slightest hesitation in the mind of the reader that Balaam in these passages is identical with Jesus, the following passage should forever set his mind at rest.

The Age of Balaam (Jesus).—In the Babylonian Talmud Sanhedrin 106*b* we read thus: "A certain heretic (*min*) said to Rabbi Hanina, 'Have you ever heard how old Balaam was?' He replied, 'There is nothing written about it. But

[19] Judas Iscariot would answer to Doeg the Edomite, who betrayed David (1 Sam. xxii. 9).

since it is said, Bloodthirsty and deceitful men shall not live out half their days (Ps. lv. 23), he was either thirty-three or thirty-four years old.' He (the heretic) said, 'Thou hast spoken well, I have seen the chronicle of Balaam in which it is said, Balaam, the lame, was thirty-three years old when the robber Phinchas killed him.' "

Rabbi Hanina lived at Sepphoris and died 232 A. D. There seems to be no apparent reason why a Christian (*a min*) should have asked him as to the age of the ancient Balaam. He might well have inquired about the age of Jesus. It would seem, however, that the Christian was not asking for information, but had a desire to find out whether the rabbi knew anything about Jesus. For he confirmed the rabbi's answer by facts known to himself. The "Chronicle of Balaam" probably denotes a Gospel, though none of the known Gospels states in so many words that Jesus was as much as thirty-three years old. If, however, it was believed that his ministry lasted three years, and that he was "about thirty years old" when he began to preach, the statement of the Christian is sufficiently borne out, though not verbally correct. Rabbi Hanina must have had fairly good grounds for his opinion as to the age of Jesus, or he would not have quoted a text which would only apply to the case of a man about thirty-three or thirty-four years old.

As to Phinchas the robber or "Pinchas Listāāh" who is said to have killed Balaam, it is difficult to understand why this worthy, who is mentioned in Num. xxv. 23 et seq. as having led an army against the Midianites and slain their kings together with Balaam with the sword, and this at Moses's command, should be called "the robber." Some Jewish writers see in Pinchas Listāāh a corruption of Pontius Pilate. The corruption, we admit, is a somewhat violent one; but that a Jew should call Phinchas a robber, being, as he was, a highly honored hero of tradition, must certainly be surprising. There is no doubt that under this mention of Pinchas Listāāh there lies concealed a reference to Pontius Pilate.

The Trial of Jesus.—1. In the Mishna Sanhedrin X, 11, we read: "In regard to all who are worthy of death according to the Torah, they do not use concealment against them, except in the case of the deceiver. How do they deal with him? They put two disciples of the wise in the inner chamber, and he sits in the outer chamber, and they light the lamp so that they shall see him and hear his voice. And thus they did to Ben Stada in Lud; two disciples of the wise were chosen for him, and they (brought him to the court of justice) and stoned him."

2. In the Jerusalem Recension VII, 16 (fol. 25*c, d*) we read: "The deceiver; this denotes a

private man. Not a sage? No. From the time he deceives he is no longer a sage. And from the time he is deceived he is no longer a sage. How do they deal with him to work craftily against him? They conceal (in his case) two witnesses in the inner chamber and make him sit in the outer chamber, and they light a lamp over him that they may see him and may hear his voice. Thus did they to Ben Stada in Lud, and they concealed in his case two disciples of the wise, and brought him to the court of justice and stoned him.

3. The Babylonian Gemara Sanhedrin 67*a* has the following version of this incident: "For it is a tradition that in regard to the rest of all who are worthy of death according to the law, they do not use concealment except in this case (i. e., of the deceiver). How do they deal with him? They light a lamp for him in the inner chamber and set witnesses in the outer chamber, so that they may see him and hear his voice, but he does not see them. And one says to him, 'Say to me what thou saidst to me in private,' and he says it to him. And another says to him, 'How shall we forsake our God who is in heaven, and practice false worship? If he repents, it is well. If he says, 'Such is our duty and thus it becomes us to do,' the witnesses who hear him from outside, bring him to the court of justice and stone him.

And thus they did to Ben Stada in Lud, and they hung him on the eve of the Passover."

That the case described in these passages refers to Jesus (called Ben Stada), who was also charged with deceiving the people, is clear. It is also clear that at an early period there was a tradition that the condemnation of Jesus had been obtained by the fraudulent means described above. There can be no doubt that in these passages we have here only scanty remnants of a tradition about that trial, combined perhaps with hearsay information derived from Christians. Renan in his *Life of Jesus* (chap. 24) believes that the New Testament account of the Trial of Jesus must be supplemented by these Talmudic notices. But an equally good, if not better authority, Keim (*Jesus of Nazara* VI, 47n.) says that there is no ground for correcting the Gospel account by the help of the Talmud. Rather it is the Gospel account which throws light upon the Talmudic tradition. From the Gospel story are derived the two witnesses (Matt. xxvi. 60. In Mark xiv. 56, 57, several witnesses are mentioned). The Gospel speaks of "false" witnesses, and this is perhaps the origin of the Talmudic assertion that the witnesses were concealed in order to entrap the accused. The mention of the outer and inner chamber recalls Matt. xxvi. 69, where it is said that "Peter was sitting without in the court" while the trial was going on within the house of the High Priest. The lighted lamp may have been suggested by the mention of the fire kindled in the outer court (Luke xxii. 55). And finally the statement that the accused was carried to the court of justice, may have its origin in the fact that there was, according to the Gospels, a second sitting of the council after the one at which the witnesses had been present (Mark xv. 1). The Talmudic tradition differs from the Gospel in saying that the trial took place at Lud (Lydda), and that Jesus was hung on the eve of the Passover. Of this we shall speak further on. But all tends to show that the Talmud has preserved only a very vague and confused recollection of Jesus, whose name was doubtless held in abhorrence as that of a dangerous heretic and deceiver.

The Execution of Jesus.—We read Sanhedrin 43*a*: "And it is tradition: On the eve of the Passover they hung Jeshu [the Nazarene]. And the crier went forth before him forty days (saying), '[Jeshu the Nazarene] goeth forth to be stoned, because he hath practiced magic[20] and

[20] It is certainly strange that Jesus was charged with having practiced magic, whereas magical skill was one of the qualifications necessary for a member of the Sanhedrin. Thus we read in treatise Sanhedrin 17*a*: Rabbi Jochanan says, none were allowed to sit in the Sanhedrin, who were not men of stature, men of wisdom, men of good appearance, aged, skilled in magic,

deceived and led astray Israel. Any one who knoweth aught in his favor, let him come and declare concerning him. And they found naught in his favor. And they hung him on the eve of the Passover. Ulla said, 'Would it be supposed that [Jeshu the Nazarene] a revolutionary, had aught in his favor?' He was a deceiver, and the Merciful (i. e., God) hath said (Deut. xiii. 8), 'Thou shalt not spare, neither shalt thou conceal him.' But it was different with [Jeshu the Nazarene], for he was near to the kingdom.' "[21]

In this passage we are told that Jesus was hung. With this must be combined the evidence of the

and acquainted with seventy languages, so that the Sanhedrin might not be obliged to hear through an interpreter.—That this statement is in opposition to Deut.xviii. 10-12 makes no difference with the rabbis. The commentary indeed tells us, that this magical skill was acquired in self-defence "in order to kill the magicians who trusted in their magical arts to deliver them out of the hands of the tribunal." But this explanation does not mend the matter. Magic is a thing absolutely unlawful and expressly forbidden by God. But it may well be doubted whether the members of this great council confined their magical exercitations to the killing of magicians. We find elsewhere, that the rabbis at least made other magical experiments, and have even recorded the means which they employed, for the benefit of posterity. We refer to Talmud Berachoth *6a,* where the people and all Israel are instructed in the means to see demons. The passage being too silly, we refrain from giving it.

[21] The whole of this passage is expunged from the later editions. It is given here on the authority of the MSS. and early editions set forth by Rabbinowicz. The words in [ ] are from MSS.

passages given in the former section that he was stoned. The connection between the two statements is that Jesus was stoned, and his dead body then hung upon a cross. This is clear from the Mishna Sanhedrin vi. 4: "All who are stoned are hung, according to Rabbi Eliezer. The sages say, None is hung except the blasphemer and he who practices a false worship." The corpse was hung to a cross or else to a single beam, of which one end rested on the ground, the other against a wall (same Mishnah). The Gospels, of course, say nothing about a stoning of Jesus, and the Talmudic tradition is probably an inference from the fact that he was known to have been hung. The inference would be further strengthened by the application of the text, Deut. xxi. 23, "He that is hanged is accursed of God," a text which Paul had to disarm in reference to Jesus (Gal. iii. 13). The Talmud knows nothing of an execution of Jesus by the Romans, as modern Jews claim, but makes it wholly the act of the Jews.

What is meant by the herald going forth during forty days before the death of Jesus, is hard to tell. The herald is, of course, fictitious; the number forty days may have its origin in the Gospel. The phrase that Jesus was "near to the kingdom," Laible interprets as referring to the "Roman authorities," which would explain the hesitation of Pontius Pilate to put Jesus to death.

We rather prefer the suggestion that the reference is to the supposed Davidic descent of Jesus, a suggestion made by the late Professor Delitzsch in his *Jesus and Hillel* (3d ed., 1879) where he says on page 12, note: "Mary is also called in the Talmuds a daughter of Eli, and Jesus is called (Sanhedrin 43*a*) 'related to the royal house (of David).'"

Jesus in Hell.—In the Talmud Gittin 56*b*, 57*a*, we read: "Onkelos bar Kalonikos, nephew of Titus, desired to become a Jew. He called up Titus by necromancy. He said to him, 'Who is honored in this world?' He replied, 'Israel.' 'What about joining them?' He replied, 'Their words are many and thou canst not fulfill them. Go, join thyself to them in this world and thou shalt become a leader, for it is written (Lam. i. 5), "Her adversaries have become the head." Every oppressor of Israel is made a head.' He said to him, 'What is thy punishment?' He replied. 'That which I have determined for myself. Every day my ashes are collected and I am judged; then I am burnt and the ashes scattered over seven seas.'

"He called up Balaam by necromancy. He said to him, 'Who is honored in this world?' He replied, 'Israel.' 'What about joining them?' He replied (Deut. xxiii, 6), 'Thou shalt not seek their peace or their prosperity all thy days.' He said to him, 'What is the punishment of this man?' He replied, 'By boiling pollution.'

"He called up Jesus by necromancy. He said to him, 'Who is honored in this world?' He replied, 'Israel.' 'What about joining them?' He replied, 'Seek their good, seek not their harm. Every one who injures them, (it is) as if he injured the apple of his eye.' He said, 'What is the punishment of this man?' He replied, 'By boiling filth.' For a teacher has said, 'Every one who mocks at the words of the wise is punished by boiling filth.' Come and see the difference between the sinners of Israel and the heathen prophets!' "

The object of the gruesome story contained in this passage is to show the fate of the three chief enemies of Israel, i. e., Titus, Balaam and Jesus. And although Jesus is made to regard the Jews as the chosen race, the specially beloved, the apple of Yahveh's eye, yet his punishment seems to be the severest. Whatever that punishment was we know not. At any rate it expresses a hatred towards the most hated of all hated men.

The information which we derive from the Talmudic notices of Jesus is very little if any at all. They add nothing new to the authentic history of Jesus, as contained in the Gospels. In general, though not in detail, they serve to confirm the Christian tradition, by giving independent, and indeed hostile evidence that Jesus of Nazareth really existed, a fact which has by some been called in question. But if, beyond this, the Talmudic Jesus-tradition has no value for the history of Christianity, it shows the attitude of Judaism as represented by its leaders, towards Jesus. He is the deceiver, the sorcerer, the apostate, the "Sinner of Israel"; his birth, Jewish contempt blackened into a disgrace, and his death is dismissed as the mere execution of a pernicious criminal. And thus it is to this day. To understand Jesus and his religion Judaism must divest itself of Rabbinism. Not the Talmud, but the New Testament is the real source for the history of Jesus.

PART II.

THE DISCIPLES AND FOLLOWERS OF JESUS.

IV.

THE DISCIPLES AND FOLLOWERS OF JESUS.

The Five Disciples of Jesus.—In the Talmud Sanhedrin 43*a* we read: "Our Rabbis have taught, Jesus had five disciples—Matthai, Nakkai, Netzer, Buni and Thodah. They brought Matthai (before the judges). He said, 'Must Matthai be killed? For it is written (Ps. xlii. 2): *Matthai* (= when) shall (I) come and appear before God.' They said to him, 'Yes, Matthai must be killed, for it is written (Ps. xli. 5): *Matthai* (= when) shall (he) die and his name perish.' They brought Nakkai. He said to them, 'Must Nakkai be killed? For it is written (Exod. xxiii. 7): The *Naki* (= innocent) and the righteous thou shalt not slay.' They said to him, 'Yes, Nakkai must be killed, for it is written (Ps. x. 8): In secret places doth he slay *Naki* (= the innocent).' They brought Netzer. He said, 'Must Netzer be killed? For it is written (Isa. xi. 1): *Netzer* (= a branch) shall spring up from his roots.' They said to him, 'Yes,

Netzer must be killed. For it is written (Isa. xiv. 19): Thou art cast forth out of thy grave like an abominable *Netzer* (= branch).' They brought Buni. He said to them, 'Must Buni be killed? For it is written (Ex. iv. 22): *B'ni* (= my son), my first born Israel.' They said to him, 'Yes, Buni must be killed. For it is written (Ex. iv. 23): Behold, I slay *Bincha* (= thy son) thy first born.' They brought Thodah. He said to them, 'Must Thodah be killed? For it is written (Ps. c, 1): A Psalm for *Thodah* (= thanksgiving).' They said to him, Yes, Thodah must be killed, for it is written (Ps. l. 23): Whoso sacrificeth *Thodah* (= thanksgiving) honoreth me.' "

No Christian tradition exists which specifies any five out of the Twelve as having met with such a fate. But the fact that the five were called disciples of Jesus implies that they were Christians, not that they were contemporaries of Jesus. It is possible that the story refers to the persecution of Christians under Bar Cocheba, and presents a fantastic account of some incident of that persecution. The fact that the martyrdom of these disciples is described on the same page of the Talmud on which the execution of Jesus at Lud (Lydda) is narrated, shows that it was a Jewish and not a heathenish court which sentenced the disciples. On the other hand this

Talmudic passage is one of the many curious examples of the way in which the Scriptures are applied by the rabbis. It is one of the strangest specimens of transparent fiction, and of silly trifling with the words of Scripture.

Jacob of Kephar Sama (Sechanja).—Besides the five names given above the Talmud also knows of another disciple of Jesus, Jacob of Kephar Sama, who was known for his thaumaturgic power, which no doubt led him to be placed in immediate relation with Jesus, the master of sorcery, and which in his time caused a sensation that was never afterwards to be forgotten. In the Talmud this Jacob comes before us as a performer of miracles and a teacher. For convenience' sake we divide the matter, and treat

Jacob, the Performer of Miracles. — *a.* In the Tosephta Hullin II, 22, 23 we read: "The Case of Rabbi El'azar ben Damah, Whom a Serpent Bit.—There came in Jacob, a man of Kephar Sama, to cure him in the name of Jeshua ben Pandira, but Rabbi Ishmael did not allow it. He said, 'Thou art not permitted, Ben Damah.' He said, 'I will bring thee a proof that he may heal me.' But he had not finished bringing a proof when he died. Rabbi Ishmael said, 'Happy art thou, Ben Damah, for thou hast departed in peace, and hast not broken through the ordinances of the wise; for upon every one who breaks through the fence of the wise, punishment comes at last, as it is written (Eccles. x. 8): Whoso breaketh a fence a serpent shall bite him.' "

b. In Jerusalem Shabbath 14*d* we read the same almost word for word with the addition at the end: "The serpent only bit him in order that a serpent might not bite him in the future. And what could he (Ben Damah) have said? (Lev. xviii. 5): 'Which, if a man do, he shall live in them' (i. e., not die in them)."

c. In Jerusalem Aboda Zara, 40*d*, 41*a*, we find the same as in *a* above, except that after the words "came in to cure him," is added, "He said, 'we will speak to thee in the name of Jeshu ben Pandira.' "

d. In the Babylonian Talmud Aboda Zara 27*b* we read thus: "It happened that Ben Dama, son of Rabbi Ishmael's sister, was bitten by a serpent. There came Jacob of Kephar S'khanja to heal him, but Rabbi Ishmael would not allow him. Ben Dama said, 'Rabbi Ishmael, my brother, allow me to be healed by him, and I will bring thee a verse from the Torah that this is permitted.' But he had not finished his discourse when his soul departed, and he died. Then Rabbi Ishmael exclaimed over him: 'Happy art thou, Ben Dama, for thy body is pure and thy soul hath passed away in purity and thou hast not transgressed the words of thy companions, who have said (Eccles.

x. 8): Whoso breaketh through a fence, a serpent shall bite him.' "

As to the details of the story, there is little variation among the several versions given above. In all, the Christian proposes to heal the sick man in the name of Jesus ben Pandira, but Ishmael would rather have his nephew die than have him cured through the name of Jesus.

Leaving out of sight the fanaticism of this rabbi, we can only say that our narrative confirms the New Testament which records the miracles of Jesus and his disciples.

Jacob, the Teacher. — 1. In Tosephta Hullin II, 24, we read: "The case of Rabbi Eliezer, who was arrested for *Minuth*,[22] and they brought him to the tribunal for judgment. The governor said to him, 'Doth an old man like thee occupy himself with such things?' He said to him, 'Faithful is the judge concerning me.' The governor supposed that he only said this of him, but he was not thinking of any but his Father who is in heaven. The governor said to him, 'Since I am trusted concerning thyself, I will also be in this. I said, Perhaps these societies err concerning these things. *Dismissus,* Behold thou art released.' And when he had been released from the tribunal, he was troubled because he had been arrested for *Minuth*. His disciples

[22] I. e., a leaning towards Christianity.

came in to console him, but he would not be comforted. Rabbi Akiba came in and said to him, 'Rabbi, shall I say to thee why thou art perhaps grieving?' He said to him, 'Say on.' He said to him, 'Perhaps one of the *Minim* (i. e., Jewish Christians) has said to thee a word of *Minuth* and it has pleased thee.' He said, 'By Heaven, thou hast reminded me! Once I was walking along the street of Sepphoris, and I met Jacob of Kephar Sichnin, and he said to me a word of *Minuth* in the name of Jeshu ben Pantiri, and it pleased me. And I was arrested for words of *Minuth* because I transgressed the words of Torah (Prov. v. 8): Keep thy way far from her, and come not nigh the door of her house (vii. 26), for she hath cast down many wounded.' "

2. In the Talmud Aboda Zara 16*b*, 17*a*, we read the following: "Rabbi Eliezer was seized on the charge of being a Christian. The judge said to him, 'Thou, an aged man, to busy thyself with such idle matters!' He replied, 'I admit the faithful reproof of the judge.' The latter, thinking that he referred to him, whereas he really meant God, said: 'Since you trust me you are discharged.' He went home deeply distressed, and would receive no consolation from his disciples. 'Rabbi!' cried Aquiba, 'Allow me to say something which I have learned from thee.' 'Say it,' was the reply. Hast thou not had a dispute with

a Christian, and by approving what he said, got thyself into trouble?' 'Aquiba!' said he, 'thou just remindest me of a certain incident. Once upon a time I was walking in the upper street of Sepphories, when I met one [of the disciples of Jesus of Nazareth], whose name was Jacob, a man of Kefr Sekanja, who said to me: "It is written in your law: Thou shalt not bring the hire of a whore into the house of the Lord thy God (Deut. xxiii. 18). May a sink be made with it for the high priest?" This question I could not answer. Whereupon he said to me: 'Jesus of Nazareth taught me thus on the subject. It is written, He gathered it of the hire of an harlot (Micah i. 7); that is, it came from an impure source, and it may be applied to an impure use." When I heard this explanation I was pleased with it, and on this account I was accused of heresy, because I trespassed against the word: Remove thy way far from her (Prov. v. 8; "from her," i. e., from heresy).' "

3. The same story is also found in the Midrash on Eccles, i. 8, where the reading is: "Thus has Jesus son of Pandera taught," whereas the Talmud reads: "Jesus the Nazarene."

The Eliezer here mentioned is Rabbi Eliezer ben Hyrcanos,[23] brother-in-law of Gamaliel II,

[23] See the interesting treatise of Toettermann, *Rabbi Eliezer ben Hyrcanosive de vi qua doctrina Christiana primis seculis illustrissimos quosdam Judaéorum attraxit,* Leipsic, 1877.

the grandson of Gamaliel I, the teacher of Paul. That Eliezer was a famous teacher can be learned from the fact that he is mentioned 324 times in the Mishna. Now this famous teacher acknowledges that he was pleased with an explanation given by Jesus of Nazareth. This teaching Eliezer received from a certain Jacob, one of the disciples of Jesus, and whom the Jewish historian Graetz identifies with the apostle James.[24]

The genuineness of this incident is defended by the late Jewish scholar Derenbourg in *Essai sur l'historie et la geographie de la Palestine,* pp. 357-360, although Edersheim in *Life and Times of Jesus the Messiah* I, 537, declares it to be plainly apocryphal. But there is no ground to reject the evidence of a man so well known as Rabbi Eliezer, especially as it tells against himself. The story seems to be well authenticated.

Another Christian Who Performs Miracles.—In Jerusalem Shabbath 14*d* we read: "The grandson [of Rabbi Joshua ben Levi] had something stuck in his throat. There came a man and whispered to him in the name of Jeshu Pandera, and he recovered. When he (the Christian) went out, Joshua said to him, 'What didst thou whisper to him?' He said to him, 'A certain word.' He said, 'It had been better for him that he had died rather than this had happened.' And

[24] *Gnosticismus und Judenthum,* p. 25, note 22.

it thus befell him, 'as it were an error that proceedeth from the ruler' (Eccles. x. 5)."

The meaning of the quotation from Eccles. x. 5 seems to be that the fact of the child having been cured by a Christian was a deplorable evil which could not be undone, as the command of a ruler given in error, and implicity obeyed, may result in mischief which cannot be afterwards put right. The saying is characteristic of the feeling of Jews towards Christians in the third century in Palestine.

A Christian Judge Applied To.—In the treattise Shabbath 116*a, b,* we read: "Imma Shalom was the wife of Rabbi Eliezer, and sister of Rabban Gamaliel. There was in her neighborhood a philosopher of whom report said that he would not take a bribe. They wished to have a laugh at him. So she brought him a golden lamp, and they went before him. She said: 'I wish them to apportion unto me of the property of the family.' He said to them, 'Divide it.' He (Gamaliel) said: 'We have it written: Where there is a son, a daughter does not inherit.' He (the judge) answered, 'From the day that ye were exiled from your land, the law of Moses has been taken away, and the law of the Evangelion has been given, and in it is written, "A son and a daughter shall inherit alike:"' Next day, he (Gamaliel) brought him a Libyan ass. He (the judge) said to them, 'I have looked further to the end of the book, and in it is written: "I, the Gospel, am not come to take away from the law of Moses but to add to the law of Moses," and in it (the law of Moses) is written, "Where there is a son, a daughter does not inherit."' She said to him, 'Let your light shine as a lamp!' Rabban Gamaliel said to her, 'The ass has come and trodden out the lamp.'"

Whether the story is intended to represent more than to show the venality of this judge, is difficult to say. It is also questionable whether the philosopher possessed a text of the Gospel at all. It is more likely that he quoted what seems to be a "saying of Jesus" from a defective memory, and in this perverted form the sentence passed into the Talmud.

With this last story we have exhausted all the Talmud passages collected by Dalman. But we cannot stop here, because we believe that still more can be derived from an examination of the Talmud. We mean especially the numerous sentences which in the Talmud are placed specifically in the mouth of Jewish authorities, but which might with greater correctness be ascribed to Jesus. Of this we shall speak further on. For the present we continue our notices on the followers of Jesus.

Christians Study the Scriptures.—In the

Talmud Aboda Zarah 4*a* we read the following: "Rabbi Abahu recommended Rabbi Saphra to the Christians as a good scholar. Thereupon the Christians remitted his taxes for thirteen years. But it happened that one day Rabbi Saphra was asked to give an explanation of Amos iii. 3, 'You only have I known of all the families of the earth; therefore I will punish you for all your iniquities,' adding, 'How can you suppose God to vent his wrath on one whom he addresses as his friend?' Rabbi Saphra was unable to reply. The Christians then took him, tied a rope round his head, and tormented him. When Rabbi Abahu came and found him in this plight, he demanded of the Christians: 'Why do you torment this rabbi so cruelly?' They replied, 'Did you not tell us that he was a very learned man?' To the first question we asked of him he was unable to make any answer.' 'I did, indeed,' answered Rabbi Abahu, 'say that he was a good scholar in the Talmud, but not in the Scriptures.' But how is it that you understand the Scriptures and he does not?' To this Rabbi Abahu answered: 'We who come in contact with you Christians are obliged, for our self-preservation, to study the Scriptures; because you dispute so often with us from the Scriptures, and because we know that you study them; but the other Jews, who live among Gentiles, have no need of that, as they do not dispute with them concerning the Scriptures.' "

What a gloomy picture! The Jews read the Scriptures, not because they were concerned about the "one thing needful," but only for the sake of controversy!

Another illustration of the acquaintance of the Christians with the Scriptures is contained in Talmud Yoma 40*b*: "The disciples asked Rabbi Akiba, whether, in case that the lot appointed the goat which stood on the left of the priest for a sacrifice in the Temple, the position of the goats should be changed? He replied, 'Give the Christians (*minim*) no occasion for assailing us'; or as Rashi, the commentator, explains it: 'To the disciples of Jesus of Nazareth who discourse concerning the Scriptures, that they do not say you (Jews) act arbitrarily.' "[25]

Enactments Against Christian Writings.—That the Gospels and other writings of the *Minim* (i. e., Christians) were in circulation at an early time, we see from the many enactments of the Jewish rabbis against them. At the time that the rules for keeping the Sabbath were under consideration, it was asked in the schools whether, if the Gospels and other books of the Christians should happen to fall into the fire, it would be

[25] So in the Venice edition, quoted by Goldfahn, in Graetz's *Monatsschrift*, 1873, p. 109.

permissible to rescue them from the fire, inasmuch as the name of God was written in them, and they contained numerous quotations from the Old Testament. On this matter we read Tosephta Shabbath, XIII, 5: "The Gospels and the other books of the Christians they do not save, but these are burnt in their place, they and their sacred names. Rabbi José the Galilean says, 'On a week-day one cuts out the sacred names and hides them and burns the rest.' Rabbi Tarphon said, 'May I lose my son! if they come into my hand I would burn them and the sacred names too. If the pursuer were pursuing after me, I would enter into a house of idolatry, but would enter not their houses. For the idolaters do not acknowledge Him (i. e., God) and speak falsely concerning Him. And concerning them the Scripture says (Is. lvii. 8): And behind the doors and the doorpost thou hast set thy memorial.' Rabbi Ishmael said, 'Whereas in order to make peace between a man and his wife, God says (cf. Num. v. 23): Let my name which is written in holiness be blotted out in water, how much more should the books of the Minim, which put enmity and jealousy and strife between Israel and their Father who is in Heaven, be blotted out, and their sacred names too. And concerning them the Scripture says (Ps. cxxxix. 21), Do I not hate them, O Lord, which hate thee, and I loathe them that rise up against thee. I hate them with a perfect hatred, and they have become to me as enemies. And even as men do not save them (the books) from burning, so do they not save them from falling (from a building), nor from water, nor from anything which destroys them.' "

Almost the same thing we read in Jerusalem Shabbath 15*c* and Babylonian Shabbath 116*a*. There we see that not even the strict observance of the Sabbath was to stand in the way of the instant destruction of the books of the Minim; nay, the terrible profanity of destroying the names of God which were thought to give the material on which they were inscribed a special and inviolable sanctity, was set aside, and this not only on the Sabbath, when the cutting out of them might be held to entail "work," but according to Rabbi Tarphon, even on week days.

That, according to Rabbi Akiba, those have no portion in the world to come who read in books outside the canon (i. e., books of the Minim) we have already noticed above. Nevertheless the Gospels circulated, at least the Gospel of Matthew. For whatever may be the date assigned to it by modern critics, certain it is that in some form it circulated at a very early date. In the Talmud Sanhedrin 90*b* we read that Gamaliel II (who died about the year 110 A. D.)

was asked: "How do you know that the dead will rise again?" He adduced passages in proof of the resurrection from the law (Deut. xxxi. 16), the Prophets (Is. xxvi. 19) and the Hagiographa (Song of Songs ix.) These passages were rejected as insufficient. He finally quoted the words "the land which the Lord sware unto your fathers to give them" (Deut. xi. 21). Since the fathers were dead, the passages must have promised a resurrection, when alone the land could be given to these fathers. This shows the force of the interpretation given by Jesus in Matt. xxii. 32 ("I am the God of Abraham, and the God of Isaac, and the God of Jacob! God is not the God of the dead, but of the living"), and the inference he deduced therefrom.

V.

PROTESTS AGAINST CHRISTIANS

Rapid Growth of Christianity.—On several occasions we have referred already to the intercourse between the rabbis and Jewish Christians,[26] which shows that Minuth (i. e., Christianity) had

[26] As another illustration we quote the following from *Midrash Koheleth* on Ecclesiastes, i. 8: "Rabbi Hanina, nephew of Rabbi Joshua, went to Capernaum, and the Christians bewitched him and made him ride into the town on an ass upon the Sabbath. When he returned to his uncle, Rabbi Joshua gave him an unguent which healed him from the bewitchment. But Joshua said to him: 'Since you have heard the braying of the ass of that wicked one, you can no longer remain on the soil of Israel.' Hanina went down to Babylon and there died in peace.—Farrar, who quotes this story in *Expositor,* Vol. VI. 1877, p. 423, says: "The expression 'the ass of the wicked one' is only too plainly and sadly an illusion to the ass ridden by our Lord in his triumphal entry into Jerusalem; and the suppression of the name Jesus is in accordance with the practice of only mentioning Him in an oblique and cryptographic manner.—Lowe (*Fragment of the Talmud Babli,* Cambridge, 1879, p. 71) translated for "ass" *wine*—in the Talmud both words are expressed the same—and thinks that the Christians intoxicated him with the wine of the *agapai,* which they seem to have celebrated on Friday night. More probable, perhaps, is the meaning of Delitzsch (*Ein Tag in Capernaum,* Leipsic, 1873, p. 25) who says that the "ass of that wicked" refers to the foolish preaching of the crucified.

an attractive power. In order to break its influence and to check its growth, shortly before the destruction of Jerusalem the first formal anathema was hurled by the entire Rabbinic assembly, which had met at Janmia or Jabneh, under the auspices of Gamaliel II. Thus the great Rabbi Moses Maimonides[27] (died 1204 A. D.) says: "In the days of Rabbi Gamaliel the *minim* increased in Israel, and afflicted Israel, and seduced men to turn away from God. Then when he saw that it was indispensably necessary, he instituted that imprecation in which God is besought that the minim should be destroyed, and added it to the eighteen prayers, so that the whole number now found in the Prayer Book is nineteen." Thus far Maimonides in Hilcoth Tephilla, chap. II.

From the Talmud we learn the history of the prayer which is as follows: "Simon Pakuli arranged the eighteen benedictions before Rabbi Gamaliel in the present order at Jabneh. Said Rabban Gamaliel to the sages: 'Is there none who knows how to prepare a benediction against the minim?' Then arose Samuel the Little and prepared it (Talmud Berachoth 28*b*)." This prayer, which now forms the twelfth of the so-called Eighteen Benedictions or Shemoneh Esreh[28]

[27] The Jews call him the "second Moses," whereas Moses Mendelssohn is styled the "third Moses."

[28] See my article "Shemoneh Esreh" in McClintock and Strong's *Cyclop.*

reads now: "O let the slanderers have no hope; all the wicked be annihilated speedily and all the tyrants be cut off quickly; humble thou them quickly in our days. Blessed art thou, O Lord! who destroyest enemies and humblest tyrants."

That this was not the original form is clear from the different recensions of this prayer which exist. Thus Reichardt copied from an old manuscript the following form: "Be thou not a hope to the *meshumadim* (i. e., apostates), but may the *minim,* the double-tongued, the infidels, the traitors, perish together in a moment; may the enemies of thy people Israel be speedily annihilated; mayest thou speedily destroy the kingdom of pride and rend it in pieces; mayest thou humble them speedily in these our days. Blessed art thou, O God, for thou shalt break into fragments the wicked, and humble the proud.[29] Another form is given by Dalman, "Let there be no hope for the apostates, and the kingdom of pride mayest thou destroy quickly in our days. And let the *Nazarenes* and the Christians suddenly perish. Let them be extinguished from the book of life and not be written with the righteous. Blessed art thou, O Jahve, who humblest the wicked."[30]

[29] *The Relation of the Jewish Christians to the Jews in the First and Second Centuries.* London, 1884, p. 46.

Whatever the form of the so-called *Birkath ha-minim*—as the prayer is called—may have been, its existence is attested by Epiphanius, who says that the Jews curse and excommunicate the Nazarenes three times during the day.[31] The same we also learn from Jerome[32] and Justin Martyr.[33] In spite of all stringent measures the numbers of believers increased. As many cherished the Christian faith in secret, it was enacted that in case a reader erred in one of the benedictions, he was not to be removed from the reading-desk, but in case he erred in the benediction against the *minim* he was to be removed because he was then suspected of being a *min* himself.[34]

[30] *Die Worte Jesu,* p. 299 et seq. See also *Jewish Quarterly Review,* X (1898), 654 et seq.; Bousset, *Die Religion des Judentums im neutestamentlichen Zeitalter,* 1903, p. 155 et seq.; Fiebig, *Der Mischnatractat Berachoth* (1906), p. 28.

[31] *Adversus Haeres.,* XXIX, 9 (ed. Petav., p. 124).

[32] *Ad Jesajam* V, 18-19; XLIX, 7; LII, 4 et seq. (ed. Vallarsi IV, 81, 565, 604).

[33] *Dialogus cum Tryphone,* chap. 16.

[34] Strange to say the Talmud Berachoth 29*a* records that one year after the composition of this prayer against the *minim,* its very author while before the reading-desk could not remember it and spent from three to four hours in trying to recall it to his mind without avail. He was, however, not removed. Had the author changed his mind with regard to those for whom his prayer was intended? or did he himself belong to the church? or was he already a member of the church when he composed this prayer extempore and composed it only in order to avert suspicion of being a *min* himself?

Enactments.—The influence of Christianity being felt more and more, the rabbis changed some of their ancient customs. Thus the "standing men"[35] used to fast on several days of the week, but not on Sunday. And why did they not fast on the day after the Sabbath? Rabbi Jochanan says, "Because of the Nazarenes" (Talmud Taanith *27b*). The idea is that those who fasted had not to work, and a cessation from work on Sunday might have the appearance of observing the Christian Sunday (i. e., when the Temple was still in existence).

We also read that it was proposed that the Ten Commandments, which were recited every morning in the Temple, should be recited in the synagogues throughout the land; but this was not carried into effect because of the "carping of the *Minim*" (Talmud Berachoth 12*a*), or as the Jerusalem recension (Berachoth 3*a*) explains, "because of the misrepresentation of the *Minim* that they might not say, 'These alone were given to Moses on Sinai.' "

But this was probably not the reason. The real ground seems to me to have been to avoid conforming a part of the Jewish service to the

[35] "Standing men" has reference to those Israelites who were commissioned to act as delegates, representing the nation at the Temple in Jerusalem, and because they had to *stand* near the priest during the offering of the daily sacrifice, they were called "the standing men."

Christian, and thus making the joining of the church much easier. We know not whether the first Christians recited the Ten Commandments. But may not Pliny in his letter to Trajan (*Epist.* 97) have reference to them when he writes that the Christians bound themselves by an oath, not for any guilty purpose, but "not to commit thefts, or robberies, or adulteries, not to break their word, not to repudiate deposits when called upon?" (*Sed ne furta, ne latrocinia, ne adulteria committerent, ne fidem fallerent, ne depositum appellati abnegarent.*)

Another curious example of the necessity which the Jews felt of protesting against the Christians is the following: The inhabitants of Jericho were in the habit of repeating each to himself, in a low voice, the words "Blessed be the name of the glory of His kingdom for ever and ever," after the Shema[36] (i. e., "Hear, O Israel, the Lord our God is one God," Deut. vi. 4) had been recited aloud. But, says Rabbi Abahu,[37] "it was enacted that the words should be repeated in a loud voice, on account of the carping of the Minim. But at Nehardea (in Babylon), where there are no Minim, they repeat them to this day in a subdued voice" (Talmud Pesachim 56*a*).

[36] The watchword of the divine Unity.

[37] As he was a great opponent of the Minim, there must have been some reason for the enactment.

Great care was taken that the prayers contained not the least sign of a Christian phraseology. Thus we read: "A person who, in his prayer says 'the good shall bless thee,' lo, this is a Christian manner (the way of Minuth); but if one says, 'thy mercies extend even to the birds' nests,' 'let thy name be remembered for good,' 'we praise, we praise,' he shall be silenced (Mishna Megilla IV, 9; Berachoth V. 3)."

The Mishna is the oldest stratum of the Talmud, and our passage is one of the few in the Mishna which refer directly to *minuth* or Christianity. The meaning is obscure, but it is possible that the reference is here to some ancient Christian liturgical forms. May not the words "thy mercies extend even to the birds' nests" have had reference to Matt. x. 29? Whatever the reason, the reader was silenced.

Even the dress of the person who acted as reader of the synagogue was made a test. Thus we read in Mishna Megilla IV, 8: "If a person should say, I will not go before the Ark in colored garments, he shall not do so in white ones. If he refuses to minister with sandals on his feet, he shall not do so even barefoot." To this Mishnaic injunction the Gemara remarks, that the reason for this is because such a one might belong to the Christians. Rashi, in his commentary on that passage remarks that the Christians used to pay attention to such things.

Because the Christians used to pray towards the east, doubts were expressed as to the feasibility of having the face turned eastward during prayer, and in order to protest most emphatically against the increasing heresy (i. e., Christianity), it was recommended to turn the face westward during prayer, and the Talmud Baba Bathra 25*a* states of Rav Shesheth, who was totally blind, that he ordered his servant to place him in any other but the eastward direction when he wished to pray, because the Minim turned in that direction. The commentator on this passage, Rashi, refers it to "the disciples of Jesus."

From all this is evident that the growth of the Christian Church must have been very rapid, otherwise the synagogue would not have required these measures, intended to check the advancement of the Gospel.

PART III.

SAYINGS OF JESUS

VI.

SAYINGS OF JESUS.

Talmudic Parallels.—We have noticed two sentences which are handed down in the Talmud as sayings of Jesus. One at least is expressly quoted as a saying of Jesus. We refer to the section, headed "Jacob the Teacher." It must be surprising that in such a bulky work as the Talmud, no more should be found. Thus it may seem. But it is not so. There are numerous sentences in the Talmud which are ascribed to Jewish authorities, but which belong to Jesus. This, Jewish writers will not admit. They claim, and with them writers like Renan, that the Talmud or the rabbis were copied by Jesus. Said Renan (*Life of Jesus,* p. 108): "It is sometimes supposed that the compilation of the Talmud being posterior to that of the Gospels, appropriations might have been made by the Jewish compilers from the Christian morality. But that is inadmissible." That Renan is mistaken, we shall see. A better authority than the French writer is the late Dunlap Moore, for many years a missionary among the Jews. In his article "Talmud" in the

Schaff-Herzog Encyclop, he says: "It is admitted that the Talmud has borrowed from the neighbors of the Babylonian Jews superstitious views and practices notoriously contrary to the spirit of Judaism. Why, then, may it not have appropriated Christian sentiments too?"

Canon Farrar in *Life of Christ,* II, 485 says: "Some excellent maxims—even some close parallels to the utterances of Christ—may be quoted, of course from the Talmud, where they lie embedded like pearls in a sea of obscurity and mud. It seems to me indisputable that these are amazing few, considering the vast bulk of national literature from which they are drawn. And, after all, who shall prove to us that these sayings were always uttered by the rabbis to whom they are attributed? Who will supply us with the faintest approach of a proof that (when not founded on the Old Testament) they were not directly or indirectly due to Christian influence or Christian thought?" Wellhausen (*Israelitische und jüdische Geschichte,* 1894, p. 37 note) remarks: "The Jewish scholars think that everything that Jesus said is also in the Talmud. Yea, everything and *still more.* How was he able to find out the true and eternal from this rubbish of scribism? Why did no one else do it? And is it certain when a saying is ascribed in the Talmud to Rabbi Hillel, that the Talmud is right? Could not a Gospel word have found its way into the Talmud and sail there under false colors? That the Talmud is mainly founded upon oral tradition is a mere superstition; it is based on literature and refers to literature."

We must not overlook the fact that Jesus preached to the multitudes wherever the opportunity was offered, and it was very natural, not only that his fame spread everywhere, but also that those who heard him, spread his sayings, so that they became the common property of all. Not so the Talmudic sage and proud Pharisee, who never mingled with those who were outside of his circle. Nor must it be forgotten, that the number of those who followed Jesus was not so small as is generally believed; it is estimated too low, because the followers are so grouped together that their individual numbers do not attract our notice. But with the New Testament in our hand, we find a different result. It is therefore but natural to assume that believing Christians were the means of spreading, if not the Gospels as such, at least the sayings of Jesus. But the Gospels were circulated at a very early period, as we learn from the enactments of the rabbis against them.

At the time that the rules for keeping the Sabbath were under consideration, it was asked in the schools whether, if the Gospels and other books of the Christians should happen to fall into the fire, it would be permissible to rescue them from the fire, inasmuch as the name of God was written in them and they contained numerous quotations from the Old Testament. "The Gospels and the other books of the Christians are not to be rescued from the fire;" such is the verdict (Shabbath, fol. 116, col. 1); and Rabbi Akiba, who hailed Barcoehba as the Messiah, laid it down as an injunction that whosoever read in outside books, i. e., books of the Christians, has no portion in the world to come (Sanhedrin, fol. 100, col. 2).

All this proves that the Gospels were in circulation; otherwise we can not understand the precautions against them. Such being the case, we can also understand the origin of the sayings in the Talmud which are generally adduced as proof that the New Testament borrowed from the Talmud.

That the Gospels were read by the sages of Israel is also corroborated by the fact that Hillel II, a descendant of the famous Hillel, was secretly baptized on his deathbed by a bishop. This statement is made by Epiphanius (*Haeres.* C. XXX), himself a convert from Judaism, on the authority of Joseph, Hillel's physician, who was a witness to the scene by which he was strongly impressed. The house of Hillel, or Ellel as

Epiphanius writes, was kept closely shut after his death by his suspicious countrymen at Tiberias. Joseph obtained entrance and found the Gospel of St. John, the Gospel of St. Matthew, and the Acts in a Hebrew translation. He read, believed, and was publicly baptized: he rose high in the favor of Constantine, attaining the dignity of Count of the Empire. Burning with zeal, he turned all his thoughts to the establishment of Christian churches in the great Jewish cities. Joseph, who endured much from the Jews and the Arians, is commemorated in the *Roman Martyrology* as a confessor on July 22.

Renan's notion found a supporter in the Jewish writer E. Deutsch of the British Museum, who makes the following statement in his article on "The Talmud" published in *The Quarterly Review* (October 1867): "We need not urge the priority of the Talmud to the New Testament. . . To assume that the Talmud borrowed from the New Testament would be like assuming that Sanscrit sprang from Latin, or that French was developed from the Norman words found in English."

All this sounds very nice, and so do many other things which Deutsch tells his readers in that article on "The Talmud."[38] But how it is

[38] For a refutation of Deutsch's assertion, see my article "Talmud" in McClintock and Strong's *Cyclop.*

possible that sayings attributed in the Talmud to rabbis who lived a long time after Jesus should have been borrowed by the latter, these Jewish writers do not explain. These writers pay no attention to the name of the author to whom a saying is attributed, or the time in which he lived. They are satisfied with the mere fact that it is in the Talmud. We shall not follow this bad example. From the date added to each rabbi's name, the impartial reader will be enabled to judge whether Jesus borrowed from the Talmud, or *vice versa.*

As the "Sermon on the Mount" is regarded as the most ethical part of the New Testament we will quote it with the so-called Talmudic parallels.

1. *Jesus*: "Blessed are the poor in spirit, for theirs is the kingdom of heaven" (Matt. v. 3).

Rabbi Levitas of Jabneh (2d cent.): "Ever be more and more lowly in spirit, since the expectancy of man is to become the food of worms" (Aboth 4, 4).

This saying, Edersheim (*Life and Times of Jesus,* I, p. 532) says, is exactly opposite in spirit, marking not the optimism, but the pessimism of life.

Rabbi Joshua ben Levi (A. D. 219-279): "Behold how acceptable before the Lord are the humble. While the temple stood, meat-offering and sacrifices were offered in expiation for sins committed; but a humble spirit, such a one as immolates the desires of the flesh and the inclination of the heart on the altar of his duty to his God, is acceptable in place of sacrifices, as the Psalmist says (Ps. li. 19): The sacrifices of God are a broken heart. (Sanhedrin, fol. 43, col. 2.)

But nothing is said of "the kingdom of heaven," which Christ promised to all men! The contrast is too great to believe that the teaching of Jesus was derived from Jewish sources. And, says Edersheim: "It is the same sad self-righteousness and utter carnalness of view which underlies the other Rabbinic parallels to the Beatitudes, pointing to contrast rather than likeness. Thus the Rabbinic blessedness of mourning consists in this, that much misery here makes up for punishment hereafter (Erubin, fol. 41, col. 1). We scarcely wonder that no Rabbinic parallels can be found to the third Beatitude, nor to the fourth, to those who hunger and thirst after righteousness."

2. *Jesus*: "Blessed are the merciful, for they shall obtain mercy" (Matt. v. 7).

Beribbi (3d cent.): "He who is merciful toward his fellow creatures shall receive mercy from heaven above; but he who is unmerciful toward his fellow creatures shall find no mercy in heaven" (Shabbath, fol. 151, col. 2).

3. *Jesus*: "Blessed are they which are persecuted for righteousness' sake, for theirs is the kingdom of heaven" (Matt. v. 10).

Rabbi Abahu (A. D. 279-310): "Be rather one of the persecuted than of the persecutors" (Baba Kamma, fol. 93, col. 1).

4. *Jesus*: "Whosoever shall break one of these least commandments, and shall teach," etc. (Matt. v. 19).

Rabbi (A. D. 190): "Be equally attentive to the light and to the weighty commandments" (Aboth 2, 1).

Ben Azaï (about 100-130 A. D.): "Be prompt in the performance even of a light precept" (*ibid.* 4, 2).

The rabbis were in the habit of making a distinction in the commandments, between such as they called *light* and others which they characterized as *weighty*. Jesus viewing the law of Moses in its whole extent, recognized this distinction, though differing entirely from the rabbis as to what constituted the lighter and what the weightier commandments: "Woe unto you, scribes and Pharisees, hypocrites! for ye pay tithe of mint and anise, and cummin; and have omitted the weightier matters of the law, judgment, mercy, and faith. These ought ye to have done, and not to leave the other undone" (Matt. xxiii. 23).

5. *Jesus*: "But I say unto you, that whosoever

is angry with his brother without a cause shall be in danger of the judgment," etc. (Matt. v. 29).

Resh Lakesh (A. D. 212-280): "Whosoever lifts up his hand against his neighbor, though he do not strike him, is called an offender and sinner" (Sanhedrin, fol. 98, col. 1).

6. *Jesus*: "Leave thy gifts before the altar, and go thy way; first be reconciled," etc. (Matt. v. 24).

Rabbi Eleazar ben Azariah (about 100 A. D.): "The transgression which a man commits against God, the Day of Atonement expiates; but the transgression which he commits against his neighbor, it does not expiate, unless he has satisfied his neighbor" (Yoma, VIII, 2).

7. *Jesus*: "But I say unto you, that whosoever looketh on a woman to lust after her, committeth adultery," etc. (Matt. v. 28).

Rabbi Shesheth (A. D. 285): "Whosoever looketh on the little finger of a woman with a lustful eye is considered as having committed adultery" (Berachoth, fol. 24, col. 1).

8. *Jesus*: "But let your communication be Yea, yea; Nay, nay" (Matt. v. 37).

Rabbi José berabbi Jehudah (A. D. 100-170) explains: "What is the meaning of Lev. xix. 36 'just balances, just weights, a just ephah, and a just hin,' since a hin was included in the ephah? To teach that your yea be yea, and your nay be just." Abbaye (died 338 A. D.) says: "This means that one should not say one thing with the mouth and another with the heart" (Baba Mezia, fol. 49, col. 1).

Every right-minded person will subscribe to Abbaye's dictum, but theory is one thing and practice another. At a meeting held at Lydda and presided over by Aqiba and Tarphon, decrees were enacted that a man might break the law in all points save those of idolatry, incest and murder, in order to save his life. But even on these three points some latitude was given, and Rabbi Ishmael declared it lawful in cases of extreme necessity even to simulate compliance with heathen practices. In this way was systematized the principle of mental reservation, which enabled a man to take an oath which he never meant to keep. As an instance the Talmud (Yoma, fol. 84, col 1; also Aboda Zara, fol. 28, col. 1) tells us with great complacency the following story of Rabbi Jochanan: "He went to a woman to be cured of toothache. He saw her on Thursday and Friday. Then he said, 'What shall I do tomorrow' (for he had to preach)? She said, 'You won't want it' (i e., the remedy). He: 'But suppose I do want it?' She: 'I will tell you the secret if you swear not to reveal.' Then he swore, '*Lalaha* of Israel I will not reveal it' (this she could only understand to mean: 'By the God of

Israel; I will not reveal it'). Then she told the secret, and the next day he revealed it to the congregation. But how could this be? since he had sworn her an oath? He had sworn *Lalaha* of Israel—i. e., 'To the God of Israel I will not reveal it, but I will reveal it to the congregation of Israel." But was not this profaning the name of God (inasmuch as she would think he had committed perjury)? No, for he told her at once (i. e., when he had got the recipe he told her that he had sworn *lalaha,* not *balaha,* and the oath would not hold)."

Of Rabbi Aqiba a like instance is narrated (Kalla, fol. 18, col. 2) with the remark that he swore with his lips, but made the oath void in his heart (see above I C, 2).

9. *Jesus*: "And if any man will sue thee at the law, and take away thy coat, let him have the cloak also" (Matt. v. 40).

Rabba (A. D. 320-363) to Rabba the son of Mar: "How is that popular saying: If any one ask for thy ass, give him the saddle also?" (Baba Kamma, fol. 92, col. 2).

10. *Jesus*: "Bless them that curse you" (Matt. v. 44).

Rabbi Jehudah (A. D. 120): "Be rather of the accursed than of those that curse" (Sanhedrin, fol. 98, col. 2; 99, col. 1).

11. *Jesus*: "Take heed that ye do not your alms

before men, to be seen of them" (Matt. vi. 1).

Rabbi Yanaï (A. D. 120) to a man who gave alms in such a public manner: "You had better not give him anything; in the way you gave it to him you must have hurt his feelings" (Chagiga, fol. 5, col. 1).

12. *Jesus*: "Our Father which art in heaven" (Matt. vi. 6).

This expression which is found twice[39] in the Mishna (Yoma 8, 9 and Sotah 9, 15) is certainly taken from the New Testament, since the two rabbis who use this phrase lived after the destruction of the Temple.

As to the Lord's Prayer in general, Geikie (*Life and Words of Christ*, II, p. 619) states that Gfroerer, who took special pains to search for the Lord's Prayer in the Talmud, found that it could not be traced in any measure to older Jewish sources."

Edersheim (*loc. cit.*, I, p. 536) says: "It would be folly to deny that the Lord's Prayer, in its sublime spirit, tendency, combination and succession of petitions is unique; and that such expressions in it as 'Our Father,' 'the kingdom,' 'forgiveness,' 'temptation,' and others, represent in rabbinism something entirely different from that which our Lord had in view."

[39] Or rather once, viz., Sotah, 9, 15, for in the other passage we read: "Your father which is in heaven."

The Jewish writer Hamburger in his *Real-Encyclopädie für Bibel und Talmud* (3d suppl., Leipsic, 1892, article "Evangelien," i. e., Gospels, p. 54), says: "Each (!) sentence of this prayer (i. e., the Lord's Prayer) occurs in the prayers and teachings of the Jewish teachers in the Talmud, so that the entire (!) prayer has its home on the soil of Judaism."

Hamburger overlooks the fact that prayers which are mentioned in the Talmud are not only later than the time of Jesus, but even aside from this, are vastly different from the petitions which Jesus taught. The Mishna, the oldest part of the Talmud, it is true, mentions the so-called *Shema,* which every Israelite was to repeat morning and evening. This *Shema,* i. e., "Hear O Israel," which is made a kind of confession of faith, consists of the Pentateuch passages Deut. vi. 4-9; xi. 13-21; Num. xv. 37-41. Strange to say, though this prayer is taken from the Bible, yet women, slaves and children were not obliged to recite it (Mishna Berachoth, 3, 3). As to the other prayer, *the prayer,* or the *the Shemoneh Esreh,*[40] i. e., Eighteen Eulogies or Benedictions, it belongs according to its present form to the time between 70-100 A. D., though it contains elements much older.

[40] See my article "Shemoneh Esreh" in McClintock and Strong's *Cyclop.*

We are aware that there is an entire Talmudic treatise especially devoted to the subject of prayer, namely, the first of the Talmud, entitled "Berachoth." In this the exact position, the degree of inclination, and other trivialities, not referred to by Christ, are dwelt upon at length as of primary importance. In the same treatise we have also a number of prayers by different rabbis. Let any one take up this treatise, either in the German translation of Pinner or Goldschmidt, or in the French translation of Schwab, and he will find none which can compare with the Lord's Prayer. Take as an illustration the following: "Rab Shesheth [toward the end of the third century A. D.] when he had fasted, prayed: 'Lord of the world, it is evident before thee, that at the time that the sanctuary stood, a man sinned and brought an offering; nor did they offer of it any thing but its fat and its blood, and he was forgiven. And now I have continued fasting, and my fat and my blood have been diminished. May it please Thee, that my fat and my blood which have been diminished be as if I had offered them upon the altar, and be merciful to me'" (Berachoth, fol. 16, col. 8).

More interesting, because of its similarity to the Pharisee's prayer mentioned in the Gospel of Luke xviii. 9-14, is the following of Rabbi Nechunjah the son of Ha-Kanah, which he uttered upon leaving the school of learning: "I thank thee my God, that thou hast given me my portion among those who sit in the house of learning and not among those who sit at the corners of the street. For I rise up early, and they rise up early; I rise up early to occupy myself in things concerning the law, they rise up early to occupy themselves in things which are useless. I work and they work. I work and receive a reward, they work and receive no reward. I run and they run. I run to everlasting life, and they run to the pit of destruction" (Berachoth, fol. 28, col. 2).

13. *Jesus*: "For if ye forgive men their trespasses, your heavenly Father will also forgive you" (Matt. vi. 14).

Rabba (died after 331 A. D.): "Whoever forgives the wrong done unto him, God will also forgive his sins" (Massècheth Dèrech èrez sutta, 8, 4).

14. *Jesus*: "Lay not up for yourselves treasures upon earth where moth and rust doth corrupt" etc. (Matt. vi. 19, 20).

In the Talmud (Jerusalem Peah 15*c*; Baba Bathra 11*a*) we read of Monobazus,[41] king of Adiabene on the Tigris, who with his mother Helena and his brother Izates became converts to Judaism. After wild exaggerations of his wealth,

[41] He was king in the year 61 A. D.

the narrative goes on to say that his brothers and friends came to him and said, "Thy fathers gathered treasures and added to the treasures of their fathers, but thou scatterest them." He answered, "My fathers had their treasures below, and I lay them up above; my fathers had their treasures where the hands [of men] may lay hold of them, I, where no hand can do so. My fathers' treasures yield no fruit, but I collect what gives fruit. My fathers stored away mammon, I, treasures of the soul; my fathers did it for others, I for myself. My fathers gathered them for the world, I, for the world to come."

A Jewish writer quoting what is said of Monobazus remarks with reference to Matt. vi. 19, 20: "The Talmud enjoins this moral more strikingly and practically by attributing it to the benevolent proselyte Munbaz (=Monobazus).—But who will vouch that the words put into the mouth of this proselyte from heathenism, were not the after-thought of some rabbi? Is it possible to imagine that Jesus should have heard of his supposed words and perused them at the beginning of his ministry? *Credat Judaeus Apella!*

15. *Jesus*: "Behold the fowls of the air, for they sow not, neither do they reap," etc. (Matt. vi. 26).

Rabbi Simon ben Eleazar (3d cent.): "Hast thou ever seen a beast or a bird that followed a trade, and yet they are fed without toil. But these were only created to minister to me, while I was created to minister to my Maker. Was it not right, then, that I should be supported without toil? But I have marred my work and forfeited my support" (Kidushin, fol. 82, col. 2).

The late Prof. Franz Delitzsch, in his *Jüdisches Handwerkerleben zur Zeit Jesu,*[42] quotes this passage in the following connection:

"A learned Jew of the British Museum, Emmanuel Deutsch, published in 1867, in *The Quarterly Review,* an article on the Talmud, in which he endeavored to show that between Judaism and Christianity no such wide difference exists as is generally believed, since most of the pithy sayings and parables of the New Testament are not to be regarded as the original property of Christianity. The impression produced by this essay was all the deeper, the less able most of the readers were to compare the New Testament with this its glorification . . . . It would be very easy to demonstrate that the author has no idea of the essence of Christianity,. . . .that the records of Christianity are much older than their Talmudic parallels."

After quoting the above passage from the Talmud, together with Matt. vi. 26, Delitzsch goes

[42] English translation by B. Pick, *Jewish Artisan Life,* New York; Funk & Wagnalls, 1882, p. 23.

on: "Herr Deutsch draws many such parallels, avoiding with a proud air the question of priority, as if it could not be raised at all. For when did this Simon live? He lived in the time of Emperor Hadrian, full nigh a century later than Jesus! We will not, of course, insist on that account that he had drawn his maxim either direct from the Gospel of St. Matthew, which was current in the Hebrew language, or indirectly from Christian lips; but if there is such a real coincidence, it is evident here, as in almost every other case, that the saying of Jesus is the original, and that of Simon the copy. We say in *almost* every other case, but we might just as well say in *all* cases; for with the exception of Hillel, all Talmudic teachers whose maxims correspond to the words of the New Testament are of a far later date than Jesus and the records of Christianity.[43]

16. *Jesus*: "Therefore take no thought saying, What shall we eat? or what shall we drink?" etc. (Matt. vi. 31-34).

Rabbi Eliezer (died A. D. 117)[44] says: "He

[43] These words are the more important because they come from a scholar who understood the Talmud better than did Deutsch. Jewish scholars everywhere acknowledged the rabbinic learning of the late Professor Delitzsch, the well-known Hebrew translator of the New Testament.

[44] This Eliezer, surnamed the Great, had intercourse with Christians, especially with the Apostle James, and of his intercourse we read in the Talmud (Aboda Zara,

who still has bread in the basket, and saith, What shall I eat tomorrow? belongeth to those of little faith" (Sotah, fol. 48, col. 2).

17. *Jesus*: "For with what judgment ye judge, ye shall be judged" (Matt. vii. 2).

The *post-Mishnaic* teachers said: "He that judges his neighbor charitably, is himself judged charitably" (Shabbath, fol. 127, col. 2).

18. *Jesus*: "With what measure ye mete, it shall be measured to you again" (Matt. vii. 2).

Rabbi Meïr[45] (2d cent.): "With what measure a man metes it shall be measured to him from heaven" (Sanhedrin, fol. 100, col. 1).

Jesus: "Let me pull out the mote out of thine eye" (Matt. vii. 4).

Rabbi Tarphon, (A. D. 120): "It would greatly astonish me if there could be found any one in this age who would receive an admonition. If he be admonished to take the splinter out of his eye, he would answer: Take the beam out of thine own" (Arachin, fol. 16, col. 2).

Rabbi Jochanan surnamed Bar Napha (A. D. 199-279): "Do they say, Take the splinter out of thine eye, he will answer: 'Remove the beam out

fol. 17, cols. 1 and 2); see above II. B, 2, 2.—in the Midrash Mechiltha on Exod. xvi. 4 (ed. Friedmann, p. 47*b*) this saying is ascribed to Eleazar of Modiim. But he, too, lived in the 2d century A. D.

[45] See my article on Rabbis Meir and Tarphon in McClintock and Strong.

of thine own eye'" (Baba Bathra, fol. 15, col. 2).

Since this saying is found in the mouth of different rabbis, may not this indicate how very widely the sayings of Jesus had spread among the people?

Jesus: "Thou hypocrite, first cast out the beam out of thine eye, and then shalt thou see" etc. (Matt. vii. 5).

Resh Lakesh (A. D. 275): "What is the meaning of the passage, Examine thyself and search (Zeph. 2, 11)? He who will reprove others must himself be pure and spotless" (Baba Mezia, fol. 107, col. 2; Baba Bathra, fol. 60, col. 2).

21. *Jesus*: "Therefore all things whatsoever ye would that men should do to you, do ye even so to them" etc. (Matt. vii. 12).

Hillel (died B. C. 5? or 10 A. D.?): "What is hateful to thyself, thou shalt not do to thy neighbor. This is the whole law, and the rest is commentary" (Shabbath, fol. 31, col. 1).

This is the famous answer which Hillel is recorded to have given to a Gentile who came to him to be converted to Judaism whilst standing on one foot, an answer which modern Jewish writers quote with a show of self-complacency, and upon which rests the assertion of Jewish writers and men like Renan, who make Jesus an imitator of Hillel.[46]

[46] Stapfer (*Palestine in the Time of Christ*, 3d ed., New York, p. 289) says: "He (Hillel) has often been

As to the famous answer which Hillel is said to have given, he cannot be claimed as the original author, and the Jewish historian Jost tells us that the sentence which Hillel uttered was one which at that time was familiar to everybody (*Geschichte,* I, p. 259) ; and any superstructure based upon the assumption that he invented it, because he in particular used it, falls to the ground. But we must bear in mind that there is a wide interval between the merely negative rule of Hillel and the positive precept of Christ. The latter said: "Therefore all things whatsoever ye would that men should do to you, do ye even so to them; for this is the law and the prophets" (Matt. vii. 12; Luke vi. 31). Hillel said: "What is hateful to thee, do not to another. This is the whole law, all else is only its explanation." The Jewish writer Hamburger (in his *Real-Encyc.,* II, p.

regarded as a forerunner of Christianity, for which he is supposed to have prepared the way. We have ourselves spoken of him under this aspect, but as we now deem, erroneously. Our views have become modified." On p. 297 Stapfer remarks: "With Hillel, the 'neighbor' could be no other than a Jew. It never entered the mind of an Israelite of the first century that a Gentile or Samaritan could be in any sense a neighbor. Jesus was the first who dared to call the hated Samaritan 'neighbor,' and the spectacle which the churches formed by St. Paul presented twenty years later, when Jew and Gentile sat together at the table of the Lord, was a thing absolutely new. When Jesus said, 'All ye are brethren,' He founded a universal brotherhood of which Hillel had never dreamed."—Thus Stapfer, the French Protestant university teacher and countryman of Renan.

411) makes the remarkable admission that the negative form was chosen to make the commandment "possible" and "practical." But this is only a subterfuge. For as Edersheim correctly remarks (*loc. cit.* I, 535): "The merest beginner in logic must perceive that there is a vast difference between this negative injunction prohibiting us from doing to others what is hateful to ourselves, and the positive direction to do unto others as we would have them do unto us. The one does not rise above the standpoint of the law, being as yet far from that love which would lavish on others the good we ourselves desire; while the Christian saying embodies the nearest approach to absolute love of which human nature is capable, making that the test of our conduct to others which we ourselves desire to possess. And be it observed, the Lord does not put self-love as the principle of our conduct, but only as its ready test."

Another point is that similar sayings are found long before Hillel. Thus Diogenes Laertius relates that Aristotle (died after 322 B. C.), when asked how we ought to conduct ourselves toward our friends, answered: "As we would wish they would carry themselves toward us." And Isocrates, who lived four hundred years before the publication of the Gospel, said:

ἃ πάσχοντες ὑφ᾽ ἑτέρων ὀργίσετε ταῦτα τοῖς ἄλλοις μὴ ποιεῖτε,

i. e., "we must not do to others that which would cause anger if it were done to ourselves." In the apocryphal book of Tobit we read (iv. 15):

ἃ μισεῖς μηδενὶ ποιήσῃς,

i. e., "Do to no man that which thou hatest."

In the so-called Epistle of Aristeas, which purports to give a history of the origin of the translation of the Old Testament into Greek or the Septuagint, the same idea is put into the mouth of one of the Jewish sages, who, to the question of the king, What is the teaching of wisdom? explains: "If you who wish not that evil befall you, but rather everything good, do the same to your subjects, and to those who err, and reprimand the good men mildly."

22. *Jesus*: "Therefore whosoever heareth these sayings of mine, and doeth them, I will liken him unto a wise man which built his house upon a rock" etc. (Matt. vii. 24-27).

Rabbi Eliezer ben Azariah (about A. D. 82): "He whose knowledge surpasses his good deeds may be compared to a tree with many branches and a scanty root—every wind shakes and uproots it. But he whose good deeds excel his knowledge may be compared to a tree with a few branches and strong roots; if all the hurricanes of the world should come and storm against it they would not move it from the place" (Pirke Aboth, 3, 17).

Elisha ben Abuyah[47] (about A. D. 138): "A man who studies the law, and acts in accordance with its commandments, is likened unto a man who builds a house the foundation of which is made of freestone and the superstructure of bricks. Storm and flood cannot injure the house. But he who studies the law but is destitute of good actions, is like unto the man who builds the foundation of his house of brick and mortar, and raises the upper stories with solid stone. The flood will soon undermine and overturn the house" (Aboth de Rabba Nathan, ch. 24).

Besides these passages from the Sermon on the Mount, we will quote a few others with their respective parallels.

23. *Jesus*: "The harvest is plenteous, but the laborers are few," etc. (Matt. ix. 37).

Rabbi Tarphon (about A. D. 120): "The day is short and the task is great, and the workmen are sluggish, and the reward is great, and the Master of the house is urgent" (Aboth, 2, 15).

24. *Jesus:* "Freely ye have received, freely give" (Matt. x. 8).

Samuel (died 257 A. D.): "Behold I have taught you statutes and judgments, even as the Lord my God commandeth me (Deut. iv. 5). As

[47] See my article on this interesting rabbi in McClintock and Strong's *Cyclop.*, 2d supplement.

I have taught you freely, so teach you freely" (Nedarim, fol. 47, col. 1).

25. *Jesus* relates the parable of the marriage-feast of the king's son and the wedding garment (Matt. xxii. 1-14).

This parable seems almost transferred into Jewish tradition. Thus we read (Shabbath, fol. 153, col. 1) that Rabbi Jochanan ben Zaccaï (flourished after the destruction of the Temple) said: "It is like a king who invited his servants to a banquet, but did not appoint the time. The wise among them adorned themselves and waited at the entrance of the king's palace, saying: Can there be anything wanting at the king's house (which may delay the banquet)? But the foolish among them went after their work, saying: Can there be a banquet without preparation? Suddenly the king asked for his servants, when the wise among them entered adorned, but the foolish came into his presence soiled. The king rejoiced to meet the wise servants but was angry with the foolish servants. Let those, said he, who have adorned themselves for the banquet sit down to eat and drink, but let those who have not adorned themselves for the banquet stand and look on."

May not this rabbi have had in mind the Parable of the Ten Virgins?

26. *Jesus*: "For in the resurrection they neither

marry nor are given in marriage, but are as the angels of God in heaven" (Matt. xxii. 30).

Rab (died 247 A. D.): "In the world to come there is neither eating nor drinking, neither fruitfulness nor increase, neither trade nor business, neither envy, hatred, nor strife; but the righteous sit with their crowns on their heads, and feast themselves on the splendor of the Shechinah, as it is written (Exod. xxiv. 11): They saw God, and did eat and drink" (Berachoth, fol. 17, col. 1).

This reads like a rabbinic adaptation of the saying of Christ.

27. *Jesus*: "And whosoever shall exalt himself shall be abased; and he that shall humble himself shall be exalted" (Matt. xxiii. 12).

Rabbi Jeremiah (died A. D. 250): "Whosoever makes himself little in this world for the sake of the word of the law will be made great in the world to come, and whosoever makes himself a slave in this world for the sake of the word of the law will be made free in the world to come" (Baba Meziah, fol. 85, col. 2).

28. *Jesus*: "The Sabbath was made for man, and not man for the Sabbath" (Mark ii. 27).

Rabbi Jonathan ben Joseph (flourished after the destruction of the Temple): "It is written, Ye shall keep the Sabbath, therefore, for it is holy unto you (Exod. xxxi. 14). It is handed over to you, not ye are handed over to the Sabbath" (Yoma, fol. 85, col. 1).

This saying reminds us forcibly of Christ's words, and as Stapfer, (*loc. cit.,* p. 357) justly remarks: "We cannot help asking, Is not this saying probably later than that of Christ, and suggested by it?"

From the foregoing parallels it will be evident that the claim that the New Testament copied the Talmud must accordingly be stigmatized once for all as a vain glorification of modern Judaism, which, on the one hand, rejects the Talmud as a religious code, but, on the other, makes use of it for controversial purposes. What are the inevitable conclusions from the facts? It is clear that the sayings of Jesus are the original, and the supposed parallels the copy. If it were not so, how comes it that not all that is in the Gospels can be traced back to Talmudic sources? Says Geikie (*Life and Words of Christ,* New York, 1881): "There has been of late a tendency to exalt the Talmud at the expense of the New Testament; but let any one take up a translation of any part of it, and the exaggeration of such an estimate will at once be seen." Dunlop Moore, the author of the article "Talmud" (in the *Schaff-Herzog Encyclop.*) says: "It is admitted, too, that the Talmud has borrowed from the neighbors of the Babylonian Jews superstitious views and practices notoriously contradictory to the spirit of Judaism. Why, then, may it not have appropriated Christian sentences also?" And says Farrar concerning these so-called parallels: "Who will supply us with the faintest approach to a proof that, when not founded in the Old Testament, they were not directly or indirectly due to Christian influence or Christian thought?" (*Life of Christ,* II, 485).

Even if we assume that Jesus and His apostles borrowed from the rabbis all the expressions that occur both in the New Testament and in the Talmud, it does not prove anything. The Gospel of Jesus remains an altogether new thing, and the spiritual life that He awakened is still diametrically opposed, in many respects, to the religious life that the Talmud fosters.

INDEX

INDEX

INDEX